Fashion, Costume, *and* Culture

Clothing, Headwear, Body Decorations, and Footwear through the Ages

Fashion, Costume, *and* Culture

Clothing, Headwear, Body Decorations, and Footwear through the Ages

Volume 5:
**Modern World Part II:
1946 – 2003**

SARA PENDERGAST AND TOM PENDERGAST

SARAH HERMSEN, *Project Editor*

THOMSON

GALE

JACKSON COUNTY LIBRARY SERVICES
MEDFORD, OREGON 97501

Detroit • New York • London • Munich

THOMSON

★ ™

GALE

Fashion, Costume, and Culture: Clothing, Headwear, Body Decorations, and Footwear through the Ages

Sara Pendergast and Tom Pendergast

Project Editor
Sarah Hermsen

Editorial
Lawrence W. Baker

Permissions
Shalice Shah-Caldwell, Ann Taylor

Imaging and Multimedia
Dean Dauphinais, Dave Oblender

Product Design
Kate Scheible

Composition
Evi Seoud

Manufacturing
Rita Wimberley

LIBRARY OF CONGRESS CATALOGING-IN-PUBLICATION DATA

Pendergast, Sara.
Fashion, costume, and culture: clothing, headwear, body decorations, and footwear through the ages / Sara Pendergast and Tom Pendergast; Sarah Hermsen, editor.
  p. cm.
Includes bibliographical references and index.
ISBN 0-7876-5417-5 (set hardcover)—ISBN 0-7876-5418-3 (v.1 : alk. paper)—
ISBN 0-7876-5419-1 (v.2 : alk. paper)—ISBN 0-7876-5420-5 (v.3 : alk. paper)—
ISBN 0-7876-5421-3 (v.4 : alk. paper)— ISBN 0-7876-5422-1 (v.5 : alk. paper)
1. Costume—History. 2. Fashion—History. 3. Body marking—History. 4. Dress accessories—History. I. Title: Clothing, headwear, body decorations, and footwear through the ages. II. Pendergast, Tom. III. Hermsen, Sarah. IV. Title. GT511.P46 2004
391'.009—dc22

2003015852

Printed in the United States of America
10 9 8 7 6 5 4 3 2 1

Contents

∎∎∎

▪
▪
▪ *Volume 1:* The Ancient World
▪

Volume 2: Early Cultures Across the Globe

EARLY ASIAN CULTURES

■
■
■ *Volume 3:* European Culture from
■ the Renaissance to the Modern Era

THE FIFTEENTH CENTURY

THE SIXTEENTH CENTURY

■
■
■ *Volume 4:* Modern World
    Part I: 1900 to 1945

1900–18

Clothing

Headwear

Body Decorations

Footwear

■
■
■
■
■

Volume 5: Modern World
Part II: 1946 to 2003

Entries by
Alphabetical Order

■ ■ ■

‖ A

‖ B

C

D

E

F

‖ G

‖ H

I

J

▎ K

▎ L

M

N

O

P

T

U

V

W

Z

Entries by Topic Category

Clothing

▌ Headwear

▮▮ Body Decorations

‖ Footwear

Reader's Guide

■ ■ ■

Fashion, Costume, and Culture: Clothing, Headwear, Body Decorations, and Footwear through the Ages provides a broad overview of costume traditions of diverse cultures from prehistoric times to the present day. The five-volume set explores various items of human decoration and adornment, ranging from togas to turbans, necklaces to tennis shoes, and discusses why and how they were created, the people who made them, and their uses. More than just a description of what people wore and why, this set also describes how clothing, headwear, body decorations, and footwear reflect different cultural, religious, and societal beliefs.

Volume 1 covers the ancient world, including prehistoric man and the ancient cultures of Egypt, Mesopotamia, India, Greece, and Rome. Key issues covered in this volume include the early use of animal skins as garments, the introduction of fabric as the primary human body covering, and the development of distinct cultural traditions for draped and fitted garments.

Volume 2 looks at the transition from the ancient world to the Middle Ages, focusing on the Asian cultures of China and Japan, the Byzantine Empire, the nomadic and barbarian cultures of early Europe, and Europe in the formative Middle Ages. This volume also highlights several of the ancient cultures of North America, South and Central America, and Africa that were encountered by

Europeans during the Age of Exploration that began in the fifteenth century.

Volumes 3 through 5 offer chronological coverage of the development of costume and fashion in the West. Volume 3 features the costume traditions of the developing European nation-states in the fifteenth through the nineteenth centuries, and looks at the importance of the royal courts in introducing clothing styles and the shift from home-based garmentmaking to shop-based and then factory-based industry.

Volumes 4 and 5 cover the period of Western history since 1900. These volumes trace the rise of the fashion designer as the primary creator of new clothing styles, chart the impact of technology on costume traditions, and present the innovations made possible by the introduction of new synthetic, or man-made, materials. Perhaps most importantly, Volumes 4 and 5 discuss what is sometimes referred to as the democratization of fashion. At the beginning of the twentieth century, high quality, stylish clothes were designed by and made available to a privileged elite; by the middle to end of the century, well-made clothes were widely available in the West, and new styles came from creative and usually youth-oriented cultural groups as often as they did from designers.

Organization

Fashion, Costume, and Culture is organized into twenty-five chapters, focusing on specific cultural traditions or on a specific chronological period in history. Each of these chapters share the following components:

- A chapter introduction, which discusses the general historical framework for the chapter and highlights the major social and economic factors that relate to the development of costume traditions.

- Four sections that cover Clothing, Headwear, Body Decorations, and Footwear. Each of these sections opens with an overview that discusses general trends within the broader category, and nearly every section contains one or more essays on specific garments or trends that were important during the period.

Each chapter introduction and individual essay in *Fashion, Costume, and Culture* includes a For More Information section listing sources—books, articles, and Web sites—containing additional information on fashion and the people and events it addresses. Some essays also contain *See also* references that direct the reader to other essays within the set that can offer more information on this or related items.

Bringing the text to life are more than 330 color or black-and-white photos and maps, while numerous sidebar boxes offer additional insight into the people, places, and happenings that influenced fashion throughout the years. Other features include tables of contents listing the contents of all five volumes, listing the entries by alphabetical order, and listing entries by category. Rounding out the set are a timeline of important events in fashion history, a words to know section defining terms used throughout the set, a bibliography of general fashion sources, including notable Web sites, and a comprehensive subject index, which provides easy access to the subjects discussed throughout *Fashion, Costume, and Culture*.

Acknowledgments

Many thanks to the following advisors who provided valuable comments and suggestions for *Fashion, Costume, and Culture:* Ginny Chaussee, Retired Media Specialist, Mountain Pointe High School, Phoenix, Arizona; Carol Keeler, Media Specialist, Detroit Country Day Upper School, Beverly Hills, Michigan; Nina Levine, Library Media Specialist, Blue Mountain Middle School, Cortlandt Manor, New York; and Bonnie Raasch, Media Specialist, C. B. Vernon Middle School, Marion, Iowa.

No work of this size could be completed without the efforts of many dedicated people. The authors would like to thank Sarah Hermsen, who shouldered the work of picture selection and ushered the book through copyediting and production. She deserves a good share of the credit for the success of this project. We also owe a great deal to the writers who have helped us create the hundreds of essays in this book: Tina Gianoulis, Rob Edelman, Bob Schnakenberg, Audrey Kupferberg, and Carol Brennan. The staff at U•X•L has been a pleasure to work with, and Carol Nagel and Tom Romig deserve special mention for the cheerfulness and professionalism they bring to their work. We'd also like to thank the staffs of two libraries, at the University of Washington and the Sno-Isle Regional Library, for allowing us to ransack and hold hostage their costume collections for months at a time.

We cannot help but mention the great debt we owe to the costume historians whose works we have consulted, and whose names appear again and again in the bibliographies of the essays. We sincerely hope that this collection pays tribute to and furthers their collective production of knowledge.

—Sara Pendergast and Tom Pendergast

Comments and Suggestions

We welcome your comments on *Fashion, Costume, and Culture* as well as your suggestions for topics to be featured in future editions. Please write to: Editor, *Fashion, Costume, and Culture,* U•X•L, 27500 Drake Road, Farmington Hills, Michigan, 48331-3535; call toll-free: 800-877-4253; fax to 248-414-5043; or send e-mail via http://www.gale.com.

Contributors

■ ■ ■

CAROL BRENNAN. Freelance Writer, Grosse Pointe, MI.

ROB EDELMAN. Instructor, State University of New York at Albany. Author, *Baseball on the Web* (1997) and *The Great Baseball Films* (1994). Co-author, *Matthau: A Life* (2002); *Meet the Mertzes* (1999); and *Angela Lansbury: A Life on Stage and Screen* (1996). Contributing editor, *Leonard Maltin's Move & Video Guide, Leonard Maltin's Movie Encyclopedia,* and *Leonard Maltin's Family Viewing Guide.* Contributing writer, *International Dictionary of Films and Filmmakers* (2000); *St. James Encyclopedia of Popular Culture* (2000); *Women Filmmakers & Their Films* (1998); *The Political Companion to American Film* (1994); and *Total Baseball* (1989). Film commentator, WAMC (Northeast) Public Radio.

TINA GIANOULIS. Freelance Writer. Contributing writer, *World War I Reference Library* (2002); *Constitutional Amendments: From Freedom of Speech to Flag Burning* (2001); *International Dictionary of Films and Filmmakers* (2000); *St. James Encyclopedia of Popular Culture* (2000); and mystories.com, a daytime drama Web site (1997–98).

AUDREY KUPFERBERG. Film consultant and archivist. Instructor, State University of New York at Albany. Co-author, *Matthau: A Life* (2002); *Meet the Mertzes* (1999); and *Angela Lansbury: A Life on Stage and Screen* (1996). Contributing editor, *Leonard Maltin's*

Family Viewing Guide. Contributing writer, *St. James Encyclopedia of Popular Culture* (2000). Editor, *Rhythm* (2001), a magazine of world music and global culture.

SARA PENDERGAST. President, Full Circle Editorial. Vice president, Group 3 Editorial. Co-editor, *St. James Encyclopedia of Popular Culture* (2000). Co-author, *World War I Reference Library* (2002), among other publications.

TOM PENDERGAST. Editorial director, Full Circle Editorial. Ph.D., American studies, Purdue University. Author, *Creating the Modern Man: American Magazines and Consumer Culture* (2000). Co-editor, *St. James Encyclopedia of Popular Culture* (2000).

ROBERT E. SCHNAKENBERG. Senior writer, History Book Club. Author, *The Encyclopedia Shatnerica* (1998).

Timeline

■ ■ ■

THE BEGINNING OF HUMAN LIFE ■ Early humans wrap themselves in animal hides for warmth.

c. 10,000 B.C.E. ■ Tattooing is practiced on the Japanese islands, in the Jomon period (c. 10,000–300 B.C.E.). Similarly scarification, the art of carving designs into the skin, has been practiced since ancient times in Oceania and Africa to make a person's body more beautiful or signify a person's rank in society.

c. 3100 B.C.E. ■ Egyptians weave a plant called flax into a light cloth called linen and made dresses and loincloths from it.

c. 3100 B.C.E. ■ Egyptians shave their heads to keep themselves clean and cool in the desert heat, but covered their heads with wigs of various styles.

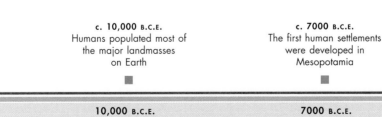

c. 10,000 B.C.E.
Humans populated most of
the major landmasses
on Earth

c. 7000 B.C.E.
The first human settlements
were developed in
Mesopotamia

10,000 B.C.E.   7000 B.C.E.

c. 3100 B.C.E. ■ Egyptians perfume their bodies by coating their skin in fragrant oils and ointments.

c. 3000 B.C.E. ■ Men and women in the Middle East, Africa, and the Far East have wrapped turbans on their heads since ancient times, and the turban continues to be popular with both men and women in many modern cultures.

c. 2600 B.C.E. TO 900 C.E. ■ Ancient Mayans, whose civilization flourishes in Belize and on the Yucatan Peninsula in Mexico, flatten the heads of the children of wealthy and powerful members of society. The children's heads are squeezed between two boards to elongate their skulls into a shape that looks very similar to an ear of corn.

c. 2500 B.C.E. ■ Indians wear a wrapped style of trousers called a dhoti and a skirt-like lower body covering called a lungi.

c. 2500 B.C.E. ■ Indian women begin to adorn themselves in the wrapped dress style called a sari.

c. 1500 B.C.E. ■ Egyptian men adopt the tunic as an upper body covering when Egypt conquers Syria.

c. 27 B.C.E.–476 C.E. ■ Roman soldiers, especially horsemen, adopt the trousers, or feminalia, of the nomadic tribes they encounter on the outskirts of the Roman Empire.

SIXTH AND FIFTH CENTURIES B.C.E. ■ The doric chiton becomes one of the most popular garments for both men and women in ancient Greece.

FIFTH CENTURY B.C.E. ■ The toga, a wrapped garment, is favored by Romans.

c. 3500 B.C.E. Beginnings of Sumerian civilization	c. 2680–2526 B.C.E. Building of the Great Pyramids near Giza, Egypt	c. 1792–1750 B.C.E. Hammurabi creates empire of Babylonia	44 B.C.E. Julius Caesar becomes Roman dictator for life and is then assassinated
■	■	■	■
4000 B.C.E.	**3000 B.C.E.**	**2000 B.C.E.**	**1000 B.C.E.**

c. 476 ■ Upper-class men, and sometimes women, in the Byzantine Empire (476–1453 C.E.) wear a long, flowing robe-like overgarment called a dalmatica developed from the tunic.

c. 900 ■ Young Chinese girls tightly bind their feet to keep them small, a sign of beauty for a time in Chinese culture. The practice was outlawed in 1911.

c. 1100–1500 ■ The cote, a long robe worn by both men and women, and its descendant, the cotehardie, are among the most common garments of the late Middle Ages.

1392 ■ Kimonos are first worn in China as an undergarment. The word "kimono" later came to be used to describe the native dress of Japan in the nineteenth century.

MIDDLE AGES ■ Hose and breeches, which cover the legs individually, become more common garments for men.

FOURTEENTH CENTURY TO SIXTEENTH CENTURY ■ Cuts and openings in garments made from slashing and dagging decorate garments from upper body coverings to shoes.

1470 ■ The first farthingales, or hoops worn under a skirt to hold it out away from the body, are worn in Spain and are called vertugados. These farthingales become popular in France and England and are later known as the Spanish farthingale.

FIFTEENTH CENTURY AND SIXTEENTH CENTURY ■ The doublet—a slightly padded short overshirt, usually buttoned down the front, with or without sleeves—becomes an essential men's garment.

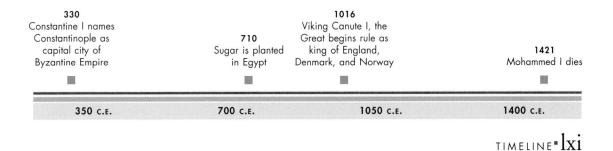

330 Constantine I names Constantinople as capital city of Byzantine Empire	710 Sugar is planted in Egypt	1016 Viking Canute I, the Great begins rule as king of England, Denmark, and Norway	1421 Mohammed I dies
■	■	■	■
350 C.E.	**700** C.E.	**1050** C.E.	**1400** C.E.

LATE FIFTEENTH THROUGH THE SIXTEENTH CENTURY ■ The ruff, a wide pleated collar, often stiffened with starch or wire, is worn by wealthy men and women of the time.

SIXTEENTH CENTURY ■ Worn underneath clothing, corsets squeeze and mold women's bodies into the correct shape to fit changing fashions of dress.

SIXTEENTH CENTURY ■ People carry or wear small pieces of animal fur in hopes that biting fleas will be more attracted to the animal's skin than to their own.

LATE MIDDLE AGES ■ The beret, a soft, brimless wool hat, is the most popular men's hat during the late Middle Ages and into the fifteenth and sixteenth centuries, especially in France, Italy, and Spain.

1595 ■ Europeans land on the Marquesas Islands in Oceania and discover native inhabitants covered in tattoos.

SEVENTEENTH CENTURY ■ The Kuba people, living in the present-day nation of the Democratic Republic of the Congo, weave a decorative cloth called Kuba cloth. An entire social group of men and women is involved in the production of the cloth, from gathering the fibers, weaving the cloth, and dyeing the decorative strands, to applying the embroidery, appliqué, or patchwork.

SEVENTEENTH CENTURY ■ Canes become carefully crafted items and are carried by most well-dressed gentleman.

1643 ■ French courtiers begin wearing wigs to copy the long curly hair of the sixteen-year-old king, Louis XIV. The fashion for long wigs continues later when, at the age of thirty-five, Louis begins to cover his thinning hair with wigs to maintain his beloved style.

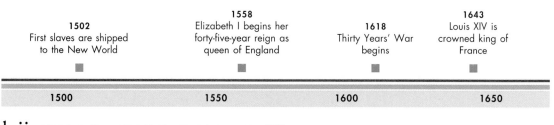

1502	1558	1618	1643
First slaves are shipped to the New World	Elizabeth I begins her forty-five-year reign as queen of England	Thirty Years' War begins	Louis XIV is crowned king of France
1500	1550	1600	1650

EIGHTEENTH CENTURY ■ French men tuck flowers in the buttonholes of their waistcoats and introduce boutonières as fashionable nosegays for men.

EIGHTEENTH CENTURY ■ The French Revolution (1789–99) destroys the French monarchy and makes ankle-length trousers fashionable attire for all men. Trousers come to symbolize the ideas of the Revolution, an effort to make French people more equal, and soon men of all classes are wearing long trousers.

1778 ■ À la Belle Poule, a huge hairstyle commemorating the victory of a French ship over an English ship in 1778, features an enormous pile of curled and powdered hair stretched over a frame affixed to the top of a woman's head. The hair is decorated with a model of the ship in full sail.

1849 ■ Dark blue, heavy-duty cotton pants—known as blue jeans— are created as work pants for the gold miners of the 1849 California gold rush.

1868 ■ A sturdy canvas and rubber shoe called a croquet sandal is introduced and sells for six dollars a pair, making it too expensive for all but the very wealthy. The shoe later became known as the tennis shoe.

1870 ■ A French hairstylist named Marcel Grateau invents the first long-lasting hair waving technique using a heated iron to give hair curls that lasts for days.

LATE 1800s TO EARLY 1900s ■ The feathered war bonnet, traditional to only a small number of Native American tribes, becomes known as a typical Native American headdress with the help of Buffalo Bill Cody's Wild West Show, which features theatrical representations of the Indians and cowboys of the American West and travels throughout America and parts of Europe.

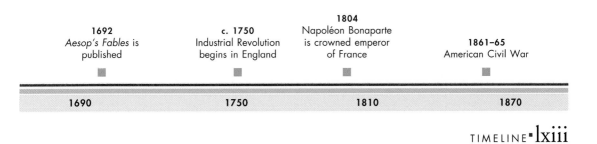

	1692 *Aesop's Fables* is published		**c. 1750** Industrial Revolution begins in England	**1804** Napoléon Bonaparte is crowned emperor of France	**1861–65** American Civil War

1690	1750	1810	1870

1900s ■ Loose, floppy, two-legged undergarments for women, bloomers start a trend toward less restrictive clothing for women, including clothing that allows them to ride bicycles, play tennis, and to take part in other sport activities.

1915 ■ American inventor T.L. Williams develops a cake of mascara and a brush to darken the lashes and sells them through the mail under the name Maybelline.

1920s ■ Advances in paint technology allow the creation of a hard durable paint and fuel an increase in the popularity of colored polish for fingernails and toenails.

1920s ■ The navy blue blazer, a jacket with brass buttons, becomes popular for men to wear at sporting events.

1920s ■ A fad among women for wearing short, bobbed hairstyles sweeps America and Europe.

1930s ■ Popular as a shirt for tennis, golf, and other sport activities for decades, the polo shirt becomes the most popular leisure shirt for men.

1939 ■ For the first time, *Vogue,* the respected fashion magazine, pictures women in trousers.

1945 ■ Servicemen returning home from World War II (1939–45) continue to wear the T-shirts they had been issued as undershirts during the war and soon the T-shirt becomes an acceptable casual outershirt.

1946 ■ The bikini, a two-piece bathing suit, is developed and named after a group of coral islands in the Pacific Ocean.

1950s ■ The gray flannel suit becomes the most common outfit worn by men working at desk jobs in office buildings.

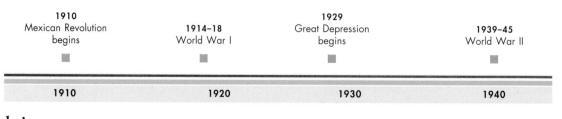

1910 Mexican Revolution begins	1914–18 World War I	1929 Great Depression begins	1939–45 World War II
1910	1920	1930	1940

1957 ■ Liquid mascara is sold at retail stores in tubes with a brush inside.

1960s AND 1970s ■ The afro, featuring a person's naturally curly hair trimmed in a full, evenly round shape around the head, is the most popular hairstyle among African Americans.

c. 1965 ■ Women begin wearing miniskirts with hemlines hitting at mid-thigh or above.

1980s ■ Power dressing becomes a trend toward wearing expensive, designer clothing for work.

1990s ■ Casual Fridays becomes the name given to the practice of allowing employees to dress informally on the last day of the work week.

1990s ■ Grunge, a trend for wearing old, sometimes stained or ripped clothing, becomes a fashion sensation and prompts designers to sell simple flannel shirts for prices in excess of one thousand dollars.

2000s ■ Versions of clothing available during the 1960s and 1970s, such as bell-bottom jeans and the peasant look, return to fashion as "retro fashions."

1947 Jawaharlal Nehru becomes the first prime minister of an independent India	1963 U.S. president John F. Kennedy is assassinated	1989 Berlin Wall falls	2001 Terrorists attack the World Trade Center and the Pentagon
■	■	■	■
1945	**1965**	**1985**	**2005**

Words to Know

∎ ∎ ∎

A

Appliqué: An ornament sewn, embroidered, or glued onto a garment.

B

Bias cut: A fabric cut diagonally across the weave to create a softly draped garment.

Bodice: The part of a woman's garment that covers her torso from neck to waist.

Bombast: Padding used to increase the width or add bulk to the general silhouette of a garment.

Brim: The edge of a hat that projects outward away from the head.

Brocade: A fabric woven with a raised pattern over the entire surface.

C

Collar: The part of a shirt that surrounds the neck.

Crown: The portion of a hat that covers the top of the head; may also refer to the top part of the head.

Cuff: A piece of fabric sewn at the bottom of a sleeve.

D

Double-breasted: A style of jacket in which one side (usually the left) overlaps in the front of the other side, fastens at the waist with a vertical row of buttons, and has another row of buttons on the opposite side that is purely decorative. *See also* Single-breasted.

E

Embroidery: Needlework designs on the surface of a fabric, added for decoration.

G

Garment: Any article of clothing.

H

Hemline: The bottom edge of a skirt, jacket, dress, or other garment.

Hide: The pelt of an animal with the fur intact.

I

Instep: The upper surface of the arched middle portion of the human foot in front of the ankle joint.

J

Jersey: A knitted fabric usually made of wool or cotton.

L

Lapel: One of the two flaps that extend down from the collar of a coat or jacket and fold back against the chest.

Lasts: The foot-shaped forms or molds that are used to give shape to shoes in the process of shoemaking.

Leather: The skin or hide of an animal cleaned and treated to soften it and preserve it from decay.

Linen: A fabric woven from the fibers of the flax plant. Linen was one of the first woven fabrics.

M

Mule: A shoe without a covering or strap around the heel of the foot.

Muslin: A thin cotton fabric.

P

Patent Leather: Leather varnished and buffed to a high shine.

Placket: A slit in a dress, blouse, or skirt.

Pleat: A decorative feature on a garment in which fabric has been doubled over, pressed, and stitched in place.

Q

Queue: A ponytail of hair gathered at the back of a wig with a band.

R

Ready-to-wear: Clothing manufactured in standard sizes and sold to customers without custom alterations.

S

Silhouette: The general shape or outline of the human body.

Single-breasted: A jacket fastened down the front with a single row of buttons. *See also* Double-breasted.

Sole: The bottom of a shoe, covering the bottom of the foot.

Straights: The forms, or lasts, used to make the soles of shoes without differentiating between the left and right feet.

Suede: Skin from a young goat, called kidskin or calfskin, buffed to a velvet-like finish.

Synthetic: A term used to describe chemically made fabrics, such as nylon, acrylic, polyester, and vinyl.

T

Taffeta: A shiny, smooth fabric woven of silk or other materials.

Textile: A cloth or fabric, especially when woven or knitted.

Throat: The opening of a shoe at the instep.

Twill: A fabric with a diagonal line pattern woven onto the surface.

U

Upper: The parts of a shoe above the sole.

V

Velvet: A fabric with a short, plush pile of silk, cotton, or other material.

W

Wig: A head covering worn to conceal the hair or to cover a bald head.

Fashion, Costume, *and* Culture

Clothing, Headwear, Body Decorations, and Footwear through the Ages

Post–World War II: 1946–60

The world woke up from a six-year-long nightmare in the summer of 1945. World War II (1939–45), which had pitted the Allied forces of the United States, Britain, France, Russia, Canada, Australia, and other nations against the Axis forces of Germany, Japan, Italy, Austria, and others, finally ended, but the effects of the war lingered on for years afterward. The economies of Europe and Japan were in ruins, and people around the world struggled to recover from the deadliest war in human history. Yet over the next fifteen years, the world did recover. Led by the United States, the economies of the world expanded and people in the West enjoyed new access to consumer goods. Meanwhile, countries such as the Soviet Union and China embraced a radical form of government known as communism. Political differences between the United States and the Soviet Union, headed by Russia, soon led to the Cold War (1945–91), and nations across the globe aligned themselves with one of the two world powers. Amid the difficulties and excitement of postwar recovery, economic expansion, and renewed conflict, people turned to fashion for relief from their worries and for ways to express themselves.

Postwar politics

Changes in world politics proved to be very important in the years after World War II. The United States and Russia were allies

Following World War II, there was an emphasis in American society on conforming to standards of dress and behavior.
Reproduced by permission of © Bettmann/CORBIS.

during the war, but that friendship would not last for long. The problem was that the two countries had very different ideologies, or ideas about how political and economic systems should work. The United States was a capitalist multiparty democracy, which meant that people had the opportunity to seek out economic gain for themselves and that all citizens had the right to elect their representatives from among several political parties. Russia, which headed an alliance of nations that came to be known as the Union of Soviet Socialist Republics, or the Soviet Union, was a Communist state. Individuals could not own property, and the profits of everyone's labor were pooled and distributed by the government, which was controlled by the Communist Party. The Soviet Union granted everyone the right to vote, but voters could only choose representatives selected by the Communist Party. In practice it was the party that controlled the state, and the people had little say.

The United States and the Soviet Union were so opposed to each other that each suspected the other of seeking to control the world. As soon as World War II ended tensions grew between the two countries, called superpowers because they were the strongest countries to emerge from the war. Both countries developed powerful nuclear weapons that they could use to destroy the other. Both countries created huge armies and posted them near each other's borders. They began to spy on each other, and they tried to convince other countries to join with them against the other. They created a world in which countries had to choose sides and join with the capitalist West or the Communists. Their conflict, which lasted until the collapse of the Soviet Union in 1991, was called the Cold War, and it dominated the world politics of the era. In the capitalist West economies boomed and people enjoyed access to a range of consumer goods, including fashionable clothes and shoes; in the Communist world people lived in very basic conditions and cared little about such luxuries as fashion. For example, in Communist China, all people were required to wear simple clothing to show that there were no differences in social class. Fashionable attire in the postwar world was only made in capitalist countries, making the West the center of fashion between 1946 and 1960.

The rise of consumerism

The United States emerged from World War II the most powerful country in the world. Though it had spent billions of dollars fighting the war, it sustained little damage. In fact the war had strengthened the United States's ability to produce goods, and the United States found the ruined economies of Europe and the rest of the world markets hungry for U.S. products. The United States created a plan to help rebuild the economies of Europe called the Marshall Plan, named after the U.S. secretary of state George Marshall (1880–1959). It provided aid to European countries in exchange for a commitment to capitalism. The United States helped Europe recover, and in turn European countries became the biggest consumers, or users, of U.S. goods.

Helping others helped the United States, and its economy boomed in the 1950s. This boom helped create a condition called consumerism, which meant that people had enough money to allow them to produce a range of goods beyond the bare necessities. Americans purchased televisions, automobiles, homes, and clothes in record numbers. They were encouraged by an advertising industry that developed a range of ways to convince people to buy their

DRESS IN COMMUNIST CHINA

For many centuries China and its clothing styles had been isolated from the rest of the world. Though some Chinese began wearing Western clothes in the early twentieth century, the vast majority of Chinese preferred traditional Chinese garb, including, among the upper classes, ornate dresses, gowns, and jewelry. By contrast the Communists who came to power in China in 1949 prided themselves on wearing standardized uniforms that showed no differences in rank or sex. Photographs of Communist leaders from the early 1940s show them wearing military-style tunics (simple shirts), trousers, and cloth peaked caps, which were essentially the same styles they would usher in upon taking control of the country at the end of the decade.

The Chinese Revolution led by the Communists in 1949 was a widespread social as well as political upheaval. Almost overnight it changed the lifestyle and clothing of people in even the most remote villages of China. Once Communist troops were established in cities, they sent in administrators to issue uniforms to workers in various industries. Factory workers and technicians were issued dark blue cotton cloth uniforms that were almost identical to the standard green Communist military uniform. Administrative and clerical workers were outfitted in gray versions of the same clothes. Men and women wore exactly the same garments. Before long

the Communist Party's grip on the country and its fashions was secure.

Chinese clothing quickly became standardized. While no direct orders were issued, it became generally understood that it was not patriotic to dress fashionably. People dressed in blue or gray cotton, padded for winter wear, and clothing made of expensive fabric was discouraged. Western-style suits disappeared almost overnight, replaced by the gray Chinese tunic suit. Women put away their stylish silk stockings and high-heeled shoes and instead put on their shabbiest clothes. Cosmetics and jewelry disappeared from view. Those who refused to comply with the new style could expect a public reprimand or a lecture from one of the local Communist Party officials.

Chinese dress was also influenced by the other major Communist nation, the Soviet Union. Women wore the fashionable Lenin suit worn by Soviet leader Vladimir Lenin (1870–1924), a jacket-and-trouser combination featuring a large turned-down collar, side buttons, and side pocket. The greatest single influence on dress in Communist China, however, was Communist Party head and supreme leader Mao Tse-tung (1893–1976; also known as Mao Zedong). From his earliest days in power, he recognized the power of dress to present a shared national identity. The shapeless four-pocketed worker's jacket he favored became the dominant dress for Chinese men and women from the 1950s to the 1970s. Dubbed the "Mao suit" in the West, it briefly found favor among political radicals in Europe and the United States.

products. Advertisements on television and radio, and in magazines continually urged Americans to purchase more and more goods. The result was the creation of what historians now call a consumer society, where the consumption of non-necessary goods and services drives the economy.

One of the biggest industries to benefit from the end of the war and the rise of consumerism was the fashion industry. People had grown tired of the clothing restrictions that governments had enacted during wartime, and soon returned to wearing luxurious and expressive clothing. New fashion trends such as the New Look and the American Look for women and the Bold Look for men offered more lavish styling and richer fabrics than had been available for years.

Clothing manufacturers who had produced millions of military uniforms for servicemen fighting in World War II had figured out how to mass-produce clothing, and in the years after the war they began to market well-made and even stylish clothes to common people. Stylish clothing once had been only for the rich, but after World War II members of the ever-growing middle class could afford good clothes. Fashion magazines like *Esquire* for men and *Vogue* for women promoted these new fashions, and giant national retailers like Sears and J.C. Penney sold them.

Conformity and rebellion

The end of one war and the beginnings of the Cold War created real stresses in American social life. Soldiers returned from the war eager to return to normal life, to buy homes, start families, and hold regular jobs. There was a national enthusiasm for a return to normality that created pressures for people to conform to standards of dress and behavior. Businessmen were happy to have a uniform, the gray flannel suit, for their daily work dress, and women embraced mix-and-match sportswear and clingy sweaters with real enthusiasm. Men wore crew cuts and women wore bouffant and beehive hairstyles. The 1950s are often simplified as a time of great conformity, a time when everybody wanted to act, think, talk, and dress the same.

By the mid-1950s, however, a growing movement away from the conformity and regularity of adult culture developed in both Europe and the United States. Teenagers in Europe and the United States began to reject the values and conventions of their parents. They listened to a new form of music called rock 'n' roll, and they adopted new rebellious clothing styles. By the late 1950s the Western world saw the emergence of a definable youth movement, and in the 1960s that movement would begin to dominate fashion.

The sweeping political and social changes of the years 1946 to 1960 had a direct relation to the fashions that people wore. From women wearing the billowy New Look dresses of 1947 to the gray-flannel-suited businessmen of the early 1950s to the dangerous-looking greasers of the late 1950s, the way people dressed reflected their attitudes about the changing social and political climate of the period.

FOR MORE INFORMATION

Anderson, Dale. *The Cold War Years.* Austin, TX: Raintree Steck-Vaughn, 2001.

Finkelstein, Norman H. *The Way Things Never Were: The Truth about the Good Old Days.* New York: Atheneum Books for Young Readers, 1999.

Gerdes, Louise I. *The 1940s.* San Diego, CA: Greenhaven Press, 2000.

Kallen, Stuart A, ed. *The 1950s.* San Diego, CA: Greenhaven Press, 2000.

Reynolds, Helen. *The 40s and 50s: Utility to New Look.* Milwaukee, WI: Gareth Stevens, 2000.

Scott, A. C. *Chinese Costume in Transition.* New York: Theatre Arts Books, 1960.

Xun, Zhous. *5000 Years of Chinese Costumes.* San Francisco, CA: China Books and Periodicals, 1987.

Clothing, 1946–60

During World War II (1939–45) fashion had taken a back-seat to the war effort, and dress designers had been severely limited in what they could make as governments placed severe restrictions on the kinds and amounts of cloth designers could use. In the fifteen years that followed the end of the war, fashions in the West went through a series of sweeping changes. Women's fashions reached levels of richness and luxury that had not been seen since the turn of the previous century. In addition, fashions across Europe and the United States highlighted women's femininity and Paris, France, reclaimed its spot as the fashion capital of the world.

In 1947 French designer Christian Dior (1905–1957) introduced a collection of women's clothes that shattered all the wartime rules. Called the New Look, this collection was most notable for its long, billowing skirts with many pleats. One of his dresses used fifteen yards of fabric. Many people were offended by the excess of Dior's collection. They felt his dresses were an insult to a world economy that was still deeply troubled after the war. But Dior's New Look soon became extremely popular. Wealthy women clamored to wear his dresses, and manufacturers soon copied his styles, introducing a range of clothing modeled on the New Look. For the next seven years, Dior's look, which included soft, rounded shoulders, a narrow waist, and accessories like gloves and umbrellas, was the single biggest influence on fashion.

Dior's New Look was part of a larger return to femininity across the Western world. The war years had forced women into unusual roles. Many worked outside the home for the first time, and the clothes they wore did not accentuate their female forms. As men returned from the war to claim jobs and start families, women also returned to more traditional roles. During the Great Depression (1929–41) and World War II women's magazines had emphasized

Teenage girls going through racks of ready-to-wear skirts. In the 1950s, young people began to wear styles quite different from those favored by their parents. *Reproduced by permission of © Jack Moebes/CORBIS.*

career advice for women, but following the war they focused much more on beauty and fashion. Advertising increased greatly and showed women how they could use makeup, accessories, and clothing to make themselves more appealing. All of these influences helped encourage women to choose more feminine clothing.

The rise of ready-to-wear

Ever since the nineteenth century Paris had dominated the world of fashion. The best designers lived in Paris. They introduced their styles, and those styles were loved and copied around the world. But when German conquerors took control of France during World War II, the dominance of Paris was interrupted. Some French designers left their country, and designers in the United States and England looked to develop fashion houses of their own. (A fashion house is the term for a small company that designs, makes, and sells high-quality clothing and accessories. It is usually associated with a single designer.) After the war the daring designs of Christian Dior,

Cristóbal Balenciaga (1895–1972), Hubert de Givenchy (1927–), and others helped refocus attention on Paris, and Paris did remain an important center for fashion. However, the emergence in the 1950s of Italian designers such as Roberto Capucci (1930–) and Simonetta Visconti, and of American designers such as Claire McCardell (1905–1958), seriously challenged French dominance of women's clothing design.

Another major challenge to the dominance of the Paris fashion houses was the rise of the ready-to-wear clothing industry controlled by large international corporations. Before the war if a person wanted well-made clothing they had to have it custom made by a tailor, and they paid a premium price. During the war manufacturers developed skills in making clothing, especially military uniforms, that allowed them to make quality clothing to fit different sizes of people. As a result regular people could now afford well-made, quality clothing called ready-to-wear, because it was purchased ready to wear without need for alterations from a tailor. Ready-to-wear clothing companies sent representatives to the major fashion shows, purchased top-quality clothing, and then made and marketed clothing lines based on high-fashion designs. This allowed common people to wear fashionable-looking clothes, but it certainly changed the fashion industry. The Paris fashion houses clothed the very wealthy, and the ready-to-wear industry provided inexpensive imitations for the masses. Before too long the designers figured out that there was more money to be made selling to the masses, and they began to develop ready-to-wear lines of their own. This was a major change in the fashion industry from the first half of the century, and it continues to this day.

Conformity and the youth explosion

One of the drawbacks of the rise of the ready-to-wear industry was that it allowed everybody to look the same. Major retail chains such as Sears and J.C. Penney sold clothes nationwide in the United States, and they didn't make major changes in their clothing lines from year to year. Also, the trend in the United States after the war was to fit in with the crowd and not cause a disturbance. These trends led to real conformity in the way that Americans dressed. People didn't want to stick out and look different, so they chose safe, conservative clothes. For businessmen this meant the gray flannel suit, the uniform of the white-collar, or business professional, worker. For women this meant a simple tight-waisted dirndl skirt and a sweater, or a range of mix-and-match sportswear. This mix-and-match look for mature women was known as the American Look. And for college students the favored look was called the Preppy Look.

While American adults valued conformity in their clothing styles, in the mid-1950s young people began to develop distinctive styles of their own. In France in the late 1940s young people calling themselves "Existentialists" dressed in shabby clothing to show their disdain for fashion. As their name implied, they existed just to exist, so clothes didn't matter so much. A similar group of Americans called themselves beats, or beatniks. Both groups favored jeans for men and women, leather jackets, and the color black. In England

BILL BLASS

Bill Blass (1922–2002), born William Ralph Blass in Fort Wayne, Indiana, is an icon of modern American fashion, famed as one of the most influential twentieth-century clothing designers. During his childhood he was charmed by such stylish 1930s Hollywood stars as Carole Lombard (1908–1942) and Marlene Dietrich (c. 1901–1992). He also was entranced by the glamorous world of New York society and expressed this fascination by drawing and sketching clothing designs. In 1940 he moved to New York to work in the city's Seventh Avenue fashion district.

Blass designed everything from sportswear to eveningwear, creating bouncy resort clothes and shapely evening gowns. While he dressed working women and housewives, his designs primarily appealed to style-conscious, upper-class American women, such as socialites, actresses, and first ladies. Nancy Reagan (1921–), wife of U.S. president Ronald Reagan (1911–), has often spoken highly of his clothes, describing them as comfortable, wearable, and pretty.

Blass favored a range of materials, including worsted woolens, a lightweight wool, crepe, cashmere, and satin. His clothes often united the traditionally masculine such as gray flannel and pinstripes, with ultrafeminine spangles and touches that conveyed 1930s glamour.

In 1967 Blass became the first American designer to create menswear along with women's clothes. His initial men's designs were on the outrageous side and even included kilts, knee-length pleated skirts. Eventually his men's creations became more conventional and more marketable.

Before Bill Blass most American fashion designers were anonymous. Manufacturer names appeared on clothing labels, rather than the individuals who created the designs. Blass changed all this. He was a charming, outgoing man and he promoted himself, circulating among and socializing with his clients and developing a public identity. Eventually, his name appeared on the labels of his clothes. This change helped to alter the identity of American fashion designers, allowing them to become brand names and celebrities in their own right. Blass, in addition, enjoyed attending the foremost New York social

stylish youths pursued the teddy-boy look, wearing long jackets with velvet collars and other extravagant outfits. By the mid-1950s, however, youth styles had gone more mainstream. The rise of rock 'n' roll music encouraged youths around the world to rebel against their parents' values, and one of the main ways they did so was through clothes. The uniform of the rebellious rocker consisted of blue jeans, a T-shirt, a leather jacket, and black boots.

The 1940s and 1950s were a fascinating time for fashion. On the one hand there were daring innovations in style, offered by big-name designers; on the other hand many people tried to look like everyone else by buying ready-to-wear clothes from major chains. It was a time when even the rebels tried to look just like other rebels, and little girls around the world took their fashion cues from a teenage fashion doll named Barbie.

events. He appeared in person at stores across the country, and he offered his name and his designs to countless charities. He donated ten million dollars to the New York Public Library and actively funded AIDS-related programs.

In 1970 Blass established Bill Blass Limited, which marketed everything from perfume to chocolate, bed linen to furniture, sunglasses to shoes, American Airlines uniforms to the interiors of Lincoln Town Cars. By the 1990s Blass had entered into almost one hundred licensing contracts, which allowed another company to sell a product he designed. His fashion empire was earning seven hundred million dollars per year. He presented his last collection in September 1999, just prior to retiring and selling his company for a reported fifty million dollars. During his last years he worked with Indiana University on a retrospective of his career. The exhibit opened after his death in 2002.

Throughout his career Blass was much honored. He won the Coty American Fashion Critics Award in 1961, 1963, and 1970. He earned the Council of Fashion Designers of America Lifetime Achievement Award in 1987 and the Humanitarian Leadership Award nine years later.

Bill Blass, great American fashion designer. *Reproduced by permission of © Bettmann/CORBIS.*

FOR MORE INFORMATION

Batterberry, Michael, and Ariane Batterberry. *Fashion: The Mirror of History.* New York: Greenwich House, 1977.

Blass, Bill, and Cathy Horyn. *Bare Blass.* New York: HarperCollins, 2002.

Laver, James. *Costume and Fashion: A Concise History.* 4th ed. London, England: Thames and Hudson, 2002.

Miller, Brandon Marie. *Dressed for the Occasion: What Americans Wore 1620–1970.* Minneapolis, MN: Lerner Publications, 1999.

Mulvagh, Jane. *Vogue History of 20th Century Fashion.* New York: Viking, 1988.

Rowold, Kathleen, Helen O'Hagan, and Michael Vollbracht, eds. *Bill Blass: An American Designer.* New York: Harry N. Abrams, 2002.

Steele, Valerie. *Fifty Years of Fashion: New Look to Now.* New Haven, CT: Yale University Press, 1997.

American Look

In fashion history the late 1940s are best known for the introduction of the New Look, a return to luxurious feminine clothes that was begun by French designer Christian Dior (1905–1957). Across the ocean, however, American designer Claire McCardell (1905–1958) was creating a revolution in fashion of her own. During World War II (1939–45), when French designers were inactive, McCardell began to design clothes that could be worn every day by busy women. In *Fashion: The Mirror of History* McCardell is quoted as saying: "I belong to a mass production country where any of us, all of us, deserve the right to good fashion." Among her first designs was a bias-cut dress. A bias-cut meant that the fabric was cut diagonally across the weave, allowing the dress to have a soft and flowing shape. McCardell also invented the popover dress, which was meant for comfortable wear around the house. Women could move easily in these dresses, and in McCardell's other designs. Observers soon hailed McCardell's designs as the American Look.

Above all else American Look clothes were simple and practical. McCardell's bias-cut dresses had adjustable waistlines and side pockets. Her dirndl skirts were slim at the waist and flared outward and could be paired with her clingy tops and light sweaters. Her ballerina leotards were stretchy and fit a variety of shapes, and she eliminated the girdle, a restrictive undergarment. McCardell was fond of simple fabrics like denim and wool jersey, a soft, stretchy woven fabric. Others soon followed McCardell's example and developed an entire range of clothing that became associated with the American Look.

The American Look had a tremendous influence on style in the United States and Europe throughout the 1940s and 1950s. Many other designers sought to make simple, comfortable women's clothes that didn't restrict movement. McCardell and others developed American Look mix-and-match sportswear, bathing suits, winter wear, coats, and other items. Interestingly, accessories like gloves and umbrellas, so important to the New Look of designer Christian Dior, were not required for a well-dressed American Look woman. The influence of the American Look's casual comfort was felt through the end of the century.

Claire McCardell designed simple, comfortable everyday clothes for the busy American woman.
Reproduced by permission of © Bettmann/CORBIS.

FOR MORE INFORMATION

Batterberry, Michael, and Ariane Batterberry. *Fashion: The Mirror of History.* New York: Greenwich House, 1977.

Mulvagh, Jane. *Vogue History of 20th Century Fashion.* New York: Viking, 1988.

[*See also* **Volume 5, 1946–60: New Look**]

Bikini

During World War II (1939–45) the United States government directed that the amount of cloth in women's beachwear be

The bikini was an aftereffect of fabric rationing during World War II, when cloth used in women's swimwear had to be reduced by 10 percent.
Reproduced by permission of © Bettmann/CORBIS.

reduced by 10 percent to conserve fabric which was needed in the war effort. As a result swimsuit manufacturers produced suits featuring bare midriffs. Such garments, however, were downright conventional when compared to what was to come right after the war, with the invention of the bikini: a skimpy, two-piece bathing suit consisting of a bra top and two reversed cloth triangles attached by a string.

The bikini was devised separately but simultaneously in 1946 by two Frenchmen, Louis Réard (1897–1984) and Jacques Heim (1900–1967). Réard, an engineer, named his creation after Bikini, a Pacific Ocean atoll, a string of coral islands, where the United States government was testing nuclear bombs. Heim, a clothing designer, named his version atome, the French word for atom, and announced that it was the world's smallest bathing suit. Réard countered his competitor by calling the bikini smaller than the world's smallest bathing suit. Both parts of his suit consisted of only thirty inches of fabric. It was in fact so tiny that no French model would wear it in public. A nude dancer finally agreed to be photographed wearing one. After a picture of her in Réard's bikini was published, she received close to fifty thousand fan letters.

At first the bikini was considered risqué and was even banned in beauty pageants and on many European beaches. Its rise in popularity was directly linked to its being worn by attractive young movie actresses. British actress Diana Dors (1931–1984) wore a mink bikini at the 1955 Venice Film Festival, and American stars Marilyn Monroe (1926–1962) and Jayne Mansfield (1932–1967) were photographed in them in the 1950s. The 1950s screen icon who most famously put on the bikini was Brigitte Bardot (1934–), a French movie star. Bardot wore it on the French Riviera and in the film *Et Dieu . . . céa la femme* (1956), also known as *. . . And God Created Woman.*

The bikini was not worn on American beaches until the 1960s, when its rise as an acceptable mode of swimwear was linked to popular culture. First, pop singer Brian Hyland (1943–) celebrated the bikini with his hit song, "Itsy Bitsy Teenie Weenie Yellow Polka Dot Bikini" (1960). The lyrics depicted a woman, wearing a bikini for the first time, who was "afraid to come out of the water" because she was embarrassed by her scanty attire. A couple of years later, it was boldly worn by Ursula Andress (1936–) in *Dr. No* (1962), the first James Bond movie. Bikinis then became the favored attire in a cycle of popular, teen-oriented sun-and-surf movies, beginning with *Beach Party* (1963). The word even was worked into the titles of a number of these films: *Bikini Beach* (1964); *How to Stuff a Wild Bikini* (1965); *Dr. Goldfoot and the Bikini Machine* (1965); *The Ghost in the Invisible Bikini* (1966); and *It's a Bikini World* (1967). Raquel Welch (1942–) wore a fur bikini playing a cavewoman in *One Million Years B.C.* (1966). By then the bikini was fast becoming a basic beach outfit.

Women favored bikinis because of their stylishness and the liberating nature of their design; wearing them provided women the opportunity to publicly display their bodies. Men liked bikinis because they showed off more of the female body.

FOR MORE INFORMATION

Alac, Patrick. *The Bikini: A Cultural History.* London, England: Parkstone Press, 2002.

Baker, Patricia. *Fashions of a Decade: The 1940s.* New York: Facts on File, 1992.

Bold Look

The Bold Look was a style in men's clothing and accessories that sought to answer the conservatism, or reserved nature, that had characterized men's dress during the Great Depression (1929–41) and World War II (1939–45). It was created by the editors of *Esquire* magazine, the most popular men's magazine of the period, in the spring of 1948, most likely as a male answer to the popular women's styles of the day, the New Look and the American Look.

The Bold Look encouraged men to make bold choices in the hats, shirts, shoes, and accessories that they wore with their suits.

For example, *Esquire* urged men to wear shirts with the "command collar," which had a wider spread than normal collars. The magazine urged men to wear boldly striped neckties tied in a Windsor knot, a wider knot, heavy gold cuff links and wide tie clasps, and snap-brim hats, felt hats that tipped up in back and down in front, with a dented crown. They even urged men to be more daring in their choice of color for their suit.

The Bold Look enjoyed just two years of popularity, in 1948 and 1949, before it was ushered out of style by the tendency of men to make very conservative choices in their formal and business wear. The 1950s became the age of the gray flannel suit when most men simply wanted to fit in, not stick out with *Esquire's* Bold Look.

FOR MORE INFORMATION

Schoeffler, O. E., and William Gale. *Esquire's Encyclopedia of 20th Century Men's Fashions.* New York: McGraw-Hill, 1973.

[*See also* **Volume 5, 1946–60: Gray Flannel Suit**]

Furs

People have worn animal furs since the dawn of time. The earliest known hunters and trappers captured and killed animals not only to provide themselves and their families with food, but to stitch together the fur—the thick, smooth, hairy coat of animal skin—to make warm clothing. People soon developed other fabrics that provided warmth, yet at certain times in human history fur became a fashion statement, indicating great wealth and luxury. A fur coat, wrap, hat, or stole might be made of the soft and luxurious furs from mink, sable, ermine, fox, or muskrat.

The 1950s saw a return of enthusiasm for furs. Following years of frugality and uniformity in clothing due to restrictions placed on clothes during World War II (1939–45), women wore furs to show off their wealth and status. The enthusiasm for furs could be seen in popular fashion magazines as well as in such movies as *The Lady Wants Mink* (1953), *Make Mine Mink* (1960), and *That Touch of*

Mink (1962). The 1950s craze for furs recalled a similar craze from the last prosperous economic time, the 1920s, which saw such movies as *Ermine and Rhinestones* (1925), *Orchids and Ermine* (1927), and *The Lady in Ermine* (1927).

Though wearing furs has long indicated wealth and a taste for luxury, some people consider killing animals for clothes to be cruel. As early as 1961 the Disney film *101 Dalmatians* depicted the villain, Cruella de Vil, as driven by a crazed desire for animal fur. By the late twentieth century a combination of increased environmental awareness and sensitivity toward animals had made wearing fur extremely controversial. Animal rights activists claim that fur-bearing animals suffer needlessly and are slaughtered just to produce a nonessential consumer product that appeals to the purchaser's vanity. Due to the controversy several celebrities and other people who wear fur have switched to fake fur.

Worn for warmth since prehistoric times, fur also makes a fashion statement about the wearer's wealth and status. *Reproduced by permission of © Joseph Schwartz Collection/CORBIS.*

FOR MORE INFORMATION

Cudlipp, Edythe. *Furs.* New York: Hawthorn Books, 1978.

Kaplan, David Gordon. *World of Furs.* New York: Fairchild Publications, 1974.

[*See also* **Volume 3, Nineteenth Century: Fur**]

Gray Flannel Suit

The 1950s were a time of conformity in the United States and in American fashion. Middle- and upper-class families by the thousands moved out of the nation's cities and resettled in suburban, or

Gregory Peck in *The Man in the Gray Flannel Suit*. In the 1950s, the gray flannel suit was the standard uniform of office workers. *Reproduced by permission of The Kobal Collection/20th Century Fox.*

residential, communities. Husbands commuted into the cities to work, while their wives raised the children and maintained the home. At the office, casual attire was forbidden. Office workers at all levels were required to dress formally. The outfit of preference for the up-and-coming corporate executive of the 1950s was the gray flannel suit: a single-breasted, three-buttoned outfit featuring narrow lapels and shoulders and tapered trousers that lacked pleats. Rounding out the look was a pale blue or white button-down collar shirt, cuff links, a conservative striped tie, and shiny black or brown leather wing-tipped shoes. A single-breasted tweed overcoat and a brimmed hat were added during colder weather and a drip-dry raincoat was worn during stormy weather.

Gray flannel suits were strictly for office workers; they were impractical for factory workers or day laborers. Because men generally are less style-conscious than women, the look of the gray flannel suit did not vary from season to season. It remained the standard businessman's uniform even after synthetic materials that were lighter and easier to launder appeared on the fashion scene in the mid-1950s.

The man in the gray flannel suit is one of the enduring images of the 1950s. Such a man is conservative and loyal to the organization for which he works. He grasps his black or brown leather briefcase and nervously glances at his wristwatch as he stands on a commuter train platform. This gray-flannel-suit state of mind was explored in *The Man in the Gray Flannel Suit,* a best-selling novel (1955) by Sloan Wilson (1920–) that was adapted into a Hollywood movie in 1956 starring Gregory Peck (1916–2003). It is the story of a New York advertising executive, trapped in the fast-paced, competitive corporate world, who undergoes a crisis of values.

FOR MORE INFORMATION

Batterberry, Michael, and Ariane Batterberry. *Fashion: A Mirror of History.* New York: Greenwich House, 1977.

Mix-and-Match Clothing

The trend during the 1950s to wear matching clothing ensembles was followed by women from every social class. After the rationing, or limiting, of fabrics during World War II (1939–45), women embraced the availability of luxuries once again. Their outfits reflected the flood of products on the market. Accessories once limited by the war were available in all price ranges. Women eagerly accented their flowing skirts with an array of hats, gloves, belts, handbags, and shoes. But by the 1950s women's desire to accessorize began to fade. To combat falling sales, manufacturers advertised a new fashion: mix-and-match clothing.

Matching ensembles became a craze among women in the United States and Europe. Women of the 1950s began obsessively matching the various pieces of their outfits, buying bags, belts, hats, gloves, shoes, costume jewelry, and even nail polish in matching colors. Designers also began creating mix-and-match outfits, enabling women to wear specially designed looks. Mix-and-match clothing styles allowed women to wear completely coordinated ensembles.

In the 1960s women began to foster their own individualized styles and shunned mix-and-match clothing. However, the legacy of mix-and-match clothing lives on in children's clothing. The Garanimals brand of children's clothing created in 1972 continues to sell mix-and-match clothing that identifies matching separates with colorful animal tags. Children can choose their own clothing outfits by matching the types of animals on the tags, confident in knowing that a shirt and pair of pants labeled with matching panda tags will look good together.

FOR MORE INFORMATION

Ewing, Elizabeth. *History of Twentieth Century Fashion.* Revised by Alice Mackrell. Lanham, MD: Barnes and Noble Books, 1992.

[*See also* **Volume 5, 1946–60: New Look**]

New Look

The New Look clothing designs for women that emerged from the studio of French designer Christian Dior (1905–1957) in 1947 put an end to the wartime styles that had dominated fashion ever since 1939. During World War II (1939-1945) designers and clothes makers had been forced to adjust their styles to wartime cloth restrictions and rationing due to lack of materials; women's clothes were close fitting, with square shoulders and short skirts. Though clothing restrictions were still in effect in France, Great Britain, and the United States in 1947, Dior's New Look collection violated all the rules of wartime fashion: his outfits had rounded shoulders; full, billowing skirts; and a narrow waist. The dresses were lined with expensive and luxurious fabrics such as cambric or taffeta and were beautifully detailed. Outfits were accessorized with a hat, often worn to one side, long gloves, and simple jewelry. As Valerie Steele wrote in *Fifty Years of Fashion: New Look to Now*: "The longing for elegance and luxury had been suppressed for the years of the war, and the New Look promised to gratify it." As Dior described it when the clothing line was introduced, the New Look was "symbolic of youth and the future."

Designer Christian Dior, creator of the New Look, showing off the raised hemline of one of his designer skirts. *Reproduced by permission of © Bettmann/ CORBIS.*

Dior had entered the fashion industry in 1938 as a designer with the French house of Robert Piguet. In 1942 he joined the house of Lucien Lelong, where he learned a great deal about dressmaking. In 1946, with the financial support of textile manufacturer Marcel Boussac, Dior launched his own design house. The New Look designs were Dior's first collection, and in the following years Dior became one of the world leaders in haute couture, exclusive and trendsetting high fashion design. He introduced several other notable women's fashion styles, including the H-line of 1954, the Y-line of 1955, and the A-line of 1956, all named for the silhouette the design gave to women. Perhaps even more notably, Dior's house set the tone for the modern fashion house by branching out to design and license a whole line of fashion accessories and perfumes for women as well as ties for men. Though Christian Dior died suddenly in 1957, his vast fashion company still exists today.

Dior's New Look clothes created an international sensation. Critics scolded the designer for ignoring the continued rationing and the economic distress of the war years. They complained that manufacturers didn't have enough cloth to make Dior's full skirts and that women didn't have enough money to buy them. One British politician claimed that the longer skirt was the "ridiculous whim of idle people," while protestors in Paris called out, "40,000 francs for a dress and our children have no milk," according to Nigel Cawthorne, author of *The New Look: The Dior Revolution*. But women and other designers disagreed. The first women to see the designs at Paris fashion shows raved that femininity had returned to women's clothes. Designers imitated Dior's look for their collections and quickly produced ready-to-wear New Look-inspired clothing lines. (Ready-to-wear refers to clothes that can be bought "off the rack" as opposed to custom designed, tailored clothing.) The New Look killed off the utility clothing of the war years and ushered in a new era in fashion. By 1948 the New Look was the dominant fashion in Paris, France; London, England; and New York, and it continued to be popular for several years.

FOR MORE INFORMATION

Cawthorne, Nigel. *The New Look: The Dior Revolution*. London, England: Reed Consumer Books, 1996.

Ewing, Elizabeth. *History of Twentieth Century Fashion*. Revised by Alice Mackrell. Lanham, MD: Barnes and Noble Books, 1992.

Steele, Valerie. *Fifty Years of Fashion: New Look to Now*. New Haven, CT: Yale University Press, 1997.

[*See also* **Volume 5, 1946–60: American Look**]

Preppy Look

One of the most enduring styles in modern American dress is the preppy style. The term preppy derives from the expensive pre-college preparatory or prep schools that upper-middle-class White Anglo-Saxon Protestant children on the United States's East Coast

Though some of its elements are considered classic, the preppy look has gone in and out of style since its introduction in the 1950s.
Reproduced by permission of Hulton Archive/Getty Images.

sometimes attend. Novelist Erich Segal, author of the best-seller *Love Story* (1970), is credited with introducing the word preppy into common usage. Segal defined a preppy as someone who "dresses perfectly without trying to ... [and] appears to do everything well without trying to." Standard items of clothing for an authentic 1960s-era male preppy included blue blazers, button-down shirts, striped ties, khaki pants, cotton Izod polo shirts with turned-up collars, tasseled loafers, crew neck sweaters worn over neat turtlenecks, and the casual sweater slung over the shoulders with the sleeve ends cuffed over one another. Many of these styles had their origins in the 1950s.

Over time children from less privileged backgrounds began to emulate the preppy look. Preppy fashions boomed in the 1980s following the publication of Lisa Birnbach's *Official Preppy Handbook* (1980), which was written to poke fun at the rich lives of privileged East Coast college students but ended up glamorizing the culture. The book included advice on how to live the preppy lifestyle, from notes on etiquette to slang phrases to what kind of pets to buy.

Along with many other 1980s fashion excesses, the preppy trend faded, though many elements of it, such as khaki pants and button-down shirts, have never gone out of style. The preppy look enjoyed a revival of sorts in the 1990s when designers like Ralph Lauren (1939–), Tommy Hilfiger (1951–), Marc Jacobs (1964–), and Luella Bartley began to incorporate aspects of preppy style into their clothes.

FOR MORE INFORMATION

Birnbach, Lisa. *The Official Preppy Handbook.* New York: Workman, 1980.

Schurnberger, Lynn. *Let There Be Clothes.* New York: Workman, 1991.

Rock 'n' Roll Style

In the 1950s a new kind of music jolted the American mainstream: rock 'n' roll, a loud, fast, liberating sound that primarily appealed to teenagers. Rock 'n' roll was an offshoot of the rural blues and urban rhythm and blues music that for years had entertained

The greaser/rock 'n' roll look, as captured in the film *The Outsiders*.
Reproduced by permission of The Kobal Collection.

and stirred the spirits of African Americans. Throughout the 1940s and early 1950s, blues was classified as "race music" and was marketed only to African Americans. Rock 'n' roll incorporated these soulful sounds to entertain audiences of white teenagers. An added influence was the hillbilly music, or white blues, that was popular mostly in the rural American South.

The song titles and lyrics of early rock 'n' roll hits, most of which were written specifically for teenage audiences, expressed the feelings of the era's young people. A fair number of rock 'n' roll songs celebrated dancing and laughing, feeling carefree and having good old-fashioned fun. The 1955 song "Rock Around the Clock" captured teens' enthusiasm for the new music. Love was another prominent theme in rock 'n' roll. Expressing the yearning for true love despite the frustrations and disappointments of romance, the song "A Teenager in Love" was perhaps the era's classic romantic lament. Yet rock 'n' roll also dealt with teenagers' coming of age, their first stabs at independence. In the song "Yakety-Yak" a teenager is nudged to complete his household chores if he wants to receive the "spending cash" that he will use to buy the latest rock 'n' roll hit and the tightest fitting T-shirt.

Elvis Presley (1935-1977) was the first enduring rock 'n' roll idol, and his look was as popular as his sound. As he performed such hits as "Jailhouse Rock," "Hound Dog," "Heartbreak Hotel," and "All Shook Up," Elvis swiveled his hips and wore wide-shouldered jackets and loose, lightweight slacks that moved with him. He radiated rock 'n' roll style and attitude with his ducktail, a favorite hairstyle of the time that he made popular, sideburns, and mock-surliness.

During the decade, the types of parentally approved and appropriate dress for teen boys consisted of loose-fitting slacks, an ironed shirt and tie, a sports jacket, and polished black or brown loafers. Haircuts were short and neat. Clean-cut preppy boys donned tan chinos, a type of pants, that ended just below the ankles, V-neck sweaters, and white buck shoes or Top-Siders, deck shoes. Their female equivalents wore saddle shoes, bobby socks, blouses with pleated skirts, or dirndl dresses, which featured lots of petticoats, and came sleeveless or with puffed sleeves. Favored hairstyles included the ponytail and bouffant, hair that was teased and combed up to stand high on a woman's head.

Teens who embraced rock 'n' roll began looking and dressing in ways that veered from the accepted norm. Teenage boys wore tight-fitting blue jeans and white T-shirts: an outfit that represented the essence of rock 'n' roll rebellion. Or they adapted the "greaser" look favoring tight T-shirts and dungarees, a type of jean, along with black leather jackets. Their hair was grown long, greased with Vaseline, and combed on both sides to extend beyond the back of the head: a style known as the ducktail, or D.A. White bucks were replaced by blue suede shoes: the name of a mid-1950s smash-hit by early rock 'n' roll icon Carl Perkins (1932–1998). Their girlfriends expressed themselves by wearing felt poodle skirts, which often featured such images as record players and musical notes attached to their fronts, or they wore short, tight skirts, stockings, tight blouses and sweaters, and an overabundance of eye shadow and lipstick. While a preppy couple who was "going steady," or seriously dating, exchanged class rings or identification bracelets, a greaser girl instead put on her boyfriend's leather jacket.

FOR MORE INFORMATION

Brunning, Bob. *Rock 'n' Roll.* New York: Peter Bedrick Books, 1999.

Fornatale, Peter. *The Story of Rock 'n' Roll.* New York: William Morrow, 1987.

Gish, D. L. *Rock 'n' Roll.* North Mankato, MN: Smart Apple Media, 2002.

Kallen, Stuart A. *The Roots of Rock: The 1950s (The History of Rock 'N' Roll).* Bloomington, MN: Abdo and Daughters, 1989.

Marcovitz, Hal. *Rock 'n' Roll (American Symbols and Their Meanings).* Philadelphia, PA: Mason Crest Publishers, 2003.

Headwear, 1946–60

The late 1940s and 1950s were a time in fashion history when many people were concerned with dressing just right, and the way they styled their hair and chose their hats was no exception. As with other areas of fashion, hat styles had been simplified during World War II (1939–45) in order to conserve precious materials that were needed for the war effort. French designer Christian Dior's (1905–1957) New Look, introduced in 1947, called for a range of accessories. Dior's New Look outfits and the many imitations that followed all featured hats chosen to match the outfit. These hats could be highly ornate, with wide brims and veils that hung around the head, or they could be as simple as a pillbox hat, a smallish, brimless round hat. It is estimated that the typical American woman in the 1950s owned four hats. Fashion-conscious women probably had many more.

Perhaps the only thing that kept women from wearing hats during the period was the need to display their carefully tended hairstyles. Throughout the 1940s Hollywood stars led the way in setting popular hairstyles. Actress Veronica Lake (1919–1973), for example, was famous for her long hair that trailed in front of one eye. Magazines tracked the hairstyles of the stars, and women went to their hairdressers to keep up with the latest styles. Hairdressers were aided in their quest to offer women perfect hairstyles by a new invention called hair spray, a sticky spray that held ornate styles in place. Beginning in the late 1950s hairdressers used curling irons and hair spray to create elaborately curled and piled hairstyles called bouffants and beehives. The era of big hair had begun.

Hats were an important part of every man's wardrobe and were worn nearly every day by men in the West. Men's hats included the homburg, the panama hat, and the porkpie hat. These hats were made of felt, straw, or man-made materials. The exact style of hats

BARBIE

During the 1950s Ruth Handler, one of the owners of the Mattel Toy Company, noticed her daughter putting dresses on her paper dolls and got the idea for making a three-dimensional fashion doll that girls could dress and undress. Mattel introduced their new doll, named Barbie after Ruth Handler's daughter, at the 1959 American Toy Fair in New York City. Barbie was popular with girls right away, though some parents worried that she looked too sexy for a child's toy. The first Barbie came wearing a black and white striped bathing suit. Soon, dozens of outfits were available for her, including a bridal gown, tennis dress, and ballerina costume. Although Barbie was marketed as a "teenage fashion model," she had many of the clothes of the ideal 1950s housewife, such as a crisp party apron for cooking and entertaining, and a fashionable Paris gown. Within the next few years, Mattel introduced Ken, Barbie's boyfriend; Midge, her best friend; and Skipper, her little sister. Each had a variety of fashionable outfits.

Barbie's image has changed frequently over the years, in an effort to keep up with changing clothing styles and the changing image of womanhood. During the 1960s she wore stylish designer suits like those worn by First Lady Jacqueline Kennedy (1929–1994), as well as miniskirts and white go-go boots. During the 1970s the clothes for "Barbie and Ken Superstars" fit right in with the glitz and glamour of the decade. By the 1980s women's liberation had affected society's view of women, and girls could choose from a wide variety of careers for Barbie, such as doctor, police officer, or astronaut, all with appropriate outfits. The eighties also saw the introduction of ethnic Barbies, such as Black, Latin, and Asian Barbie dolls. Feminists grew angry with Barbie again in the 1990s when "Teen Talk" Barbie said things like, "Math is tough," which seemingly insulted the intelligence of a woman.

Even Barbie's face and body have changed with the styles. The first Barbie dolls had heavily made-up eyes that looked to the side, but by 1961 she had a more natural look, and her big, blue eyes looked straight out. Early Barbie dolls had feet molded in permanent tiptoes for wearing high heels, but by the 1980s a Barbie with more natural feet was available. Many people had criticized Barbie's figure as being impossible for a real woman, so in 1999 Mattel introduced a doll with a more realistic shape. Like the changes in her fashions, these changes reflected the changing look of women through the decades, evolving from the made-up and glamorous look of the 1950s to the more natural look of the 1990s.

changed from season to season, varying in color, the width and bend of the brim, and the height of the crown.

Men wore a variety of hairstyles during this period. Perhaps the most popular was the crew cut, in which the hair was cut short all over, military style. By late in the period, however, young men began experimenting with longer styles, held in place with hair gels, pomades (perfumed ointments), or sprays. The more adventurous wore a jelly roll or a ducktail, two of the more elaborate male styles. Young men who carefully gelled their hair were known as greasers. Facial hair was generally not popular during this period. Some speculate that the mustache worn by German dictator Adolf Hitler (1889–1945), who led the Germans in World War II, killed the popularity of the mustache for decades in the United States and western Europe.

FOR MORE INFORMATION

Corson, Richard. *Fashions in Hair: The First Five Thousand Years.* London, England: Peter Owen, 2001.

Jones, Dylan. *Haircults: Fifty Years of Styles and Cuts.* New York: Thames and Hudson, 1990.

Lord, M. G. *Forever Barbie: The Unauthorized Biography of a Real Doll.* New York: William Morrow, 1994.

Schoeffler, O. E., and William Gale. *Esquire's Encyclopedia of 20th Century Men's Fashions.* New York: McGraw-Hill, 1973.

Steele, Valerie. *Fifty Years of Fashion: New Look to Now.* New Haven, CT: Yale University Press, 1997.

Weissman, Kristin N. *Barbie: The Icon, the Image, the Ideal.* Parkland, FL: Universal Publishers, 1999.

Woman with hair styled in a medium-sized beehive. Hair spray and rollers brought big hair to new heights with the beehive. *Reproduced by permission of Hulton Archive/Getty Images.*

Beehives and Bouffants

One of the most popular women's hairstyles of the late 1950s and early 1960s was the lavishly teased bouffant. The bouffant first surfaced in the 1950s, reflecting a return to big hair for women following a period of plain wartime styles. Two innovations of the late 1950s helped revolutionize hairstyling and paved the way for the bouffant age: the roller, used to lift and wind the hair (which was then backcombed or teased to give it maximum height); and lacquer spray, a heavy hair spray which held the style in place. Bouffants began to catch on in the United States following a *Life* magazine article touting the "aristocratic" European look. First lady Jacqueline Kennedy's (1929–1994) adoption of the hairstyle in the early 1960s helped popularize it even more.

By 1964 hair spray had become the nation's number one beauty aid, surpassing lipstick. Around that time young girls took the bouffant to new heights with a style called the beehive. Teenagers would set their hair every night in huge rollers, using a gel solution called Dippity Do, and proceed to sleep in them. Those with extremely curly hair used large frozen cans in place of the smaller rollers. Some women even wrapped toilet paper around their heads at bedtime in order to preserve the increasingly ornate, sculpted styles.

Although their popularity during the early 1960s was immense, bouffants and beehives proved difficult styles to wear, involving extensive preparation and a great number of tools. In the mid-1960s the fashion tide began to turn toward more natural hairstyles. Women who had spent hours teasing their hair just a few years earlier now began ironing it in an effort to achieve optimum straightness. The bouffant soon became a comical symbol of an earlier era. The outrageous beehive was mocked in popular culture by the flamboyant rock band The B-52s and in the film and Broadway musical *Hairspray*.

FOR MORE INFORMATION

Corson, Richard. *Fashions in Hair: The First Five Thousand Years.* London, England: Peter Owen, 2001.

Turudich, Daniela. *1960s Hair.* Long Beach, CA: Streamline Press, 2003.

Crew Cut

Also known as a G.I., or government issue, haircut, the standard crew cut is a variation on the buzz cut, a regulation haircut given to servicemen in the U.S. military in which the entire head is sheared, typically with an electric razor. In the crew cut a thick bristle of hair less than an inch long is left at the top of the head. A variation on the crew cut, in which this strip of hair is allowed to grow out and cut in a straight, flat style, is called a flat top. When the top is slightly longer and tousled, it is known as a feather crew or Ivy League cut since it was often worn by students of Ivy League schools, the American universities with the highest academic and social prestige. Outside the United States the term crew cut has a much narrower meaning, denoting a cut that is short all over (about one-fourth inch), perhaps tapered a little at the back and sides. Crew cuts gained a following in Great Britain in the 1950s.

The crew cut did not originate in the military. In fact it first gained popularity on college campuses, where college crew, or rowing, teams adopted the style to differentiate themselves from other undergraduates. The crew cut's association with these elite organizations helped make it the hairstyle of choice for those who respected authority. As self-styled rebels, nonconformists, and antiestablishment types began to adopt longer and longer hairstyles beginning in the 1960s, those who still sported crew cuts were often ridiculed as "squares," in part a reference to their angular haircuts. By the 1990s, however, those cultural divides had largely faded into the past. Short hairstyles made a comeback, led by the buzz cut but also, notably, the crew cut, now seen as a symbol of toughness and an uncompromising personal style.

Football great Johnny Unitas sporting a crew cut. *Reproduced by permission of © Bettmann/ CORBIS.*

FOR MORE INFORMATION

Cooper, Wendy. *Hair, Sex, Society, and Symbolism.* New York: Stein and Day, 1971.

Corson, Richard. *Fashions in Hair: The First Five Thousand Years.* London, England: Peter Owen, 2001.

Hair Coloring

Hair coloring dates to ancient times, when Greeks, Romans, and others altered their hair by applying soaps and bleaches. Many Romans preferred a black dye that consisted of leeks and boiled walnuts, while Saxons added such unlikely colors as orange, green, and blue to their hair and beards. The initial chemical hair coloring was produced in France in 1909. It consisted of a mixture of ammonia, hydrogen peroxide, and the chemical paraphenylenediamine.

During the post–World War II (1939–45) years, millions of American families were entering the middle class and more women had the luxury of spending money on themselves, including their hair. Initially, however, American women were reluctant to use hair dyes. Hair coloring products were purchased in stores and applied at home, or they were put on by a hairdresser at a salon. A disadvantage of home coloring was that instructions could be misread or a mishap might occur, resulting in the hair turning an unwanted or even garish color. Another downside to early commercial hair coloring products was that they smelled awful, often like rotten eggs.

In 1950 only seven out of every one hundred women colored their hair, with most doing so primarily to eliminate gray and restore their natural color. In 1956, however, the introduction of a dyeing product called Miss Clairol brought hair coloring into the mainstream. Accompanied by a well-known advertising campaign that said "Does she or doesn't she? Hair color so natural only her hairdresser knows for sure!" Miss Clairol made hair coloring very popular.

For years only small numbers of men, in particular, aging movie stars, were known to dye their locks, but the process became increasingly popular among males in the 1990s. Still, hair coloring mostly is the domain of women. In the twenty-first century over 75 percent of all American women reportedly color their hair.

FOR MORE INFORMATION

Adams, David, and Jacki Wadeson. *The Art of Hair Colouring.* London, England: Macmillan, 1998.

Gladwell, Malcolm. "True Colors." *New Yorker* (March 22, 1999): 70–81.

[*See also* **Volume 1, Ancient Rome: Hair Coloring**]

Hair Spray

After the end of World War II (1939–45), many people considered the 1950s to be the beginning of a modern world, full of new products that would make their lives easier. The bright, the shiny, and the new were valued above all, and fashions reflected this. Hair spray, made of liquid plastics and vinyl that harden when they are sprayed on the hair to form a kind of shell that keeps the hair from falling out of its style, became very popular during the 1950s and early 1960s. Styles were crisp and clean, and hairstyles were held in place with aerosol hair spray. Aerosol sprays, substances dispensed from a pressurized can, had been developed for use with insecticides during World War II, and they were quickly adopted by the hair-care industry. Women of the 1950s used products such as Helene Curtis Spray Net to hold their hair neatly in place.

By the end of the decade, hair sprays had inspired the creation of hairstyles that would have been impossible without them. The beehive, popular in the early 1960s, involved teasing the hair into a tall pile on top of the head and holding it in place with hair spray. Beehives were so difficult to style that most women just left them up overnight and reapplied hair spray the next day. The bouffant hairstyle, popularized during the 1960s by first lady Jacqueline Kennedy (1929–1994), wife of U.S. president John F. Kennedy (1917–1963), also required lots of hair spray to keep its full, puffy look.

The late 1960s and the 1970s saw the arrival of a much more natural style, with hair left long and loose. Hair spray sales dropped as stiffly styled hair became an object of ridicule. At the same time, environmentalists began to discover that the chemicals in aerosol hair sprays were damaging both the environment and the health of the women who used them. Some of these chemicals were outlawed.

The popularity of hair spray revived again in the 1980s, when punks, young fans of punk rock music, used it to lacquer their spikes and mohawks (a ridge of hair sticking straight up, running down the center of the head from the forehead to the nape of the neck) in place, and it has remained a part of many women's hair styling routine through the twenty-first century. Since the 1980s many men have begun to use hair spray products as well. However, it is the late 1950s and early 1960s that will always be identified with hair spray. A lighthearted 1988 John Waters film, made into a Broadway musical in 2002, captures the atmosphere of the early 1960s in its title, *Hairspray*.

FOR MORE INFORMATION

Hoobler, Dorothy, and Thomas Hoobler. *Vanity Rules: A History of American Fashion and Beauty*. Brookfield, CT: Twenty-First Century Books, 2000.

Turudich, Daniela. *1950s Hair: Hairstyles from the Atomic Age of Cool*. Long Beach, CA: Streamline Press, 2003.

Jelly Rolls and Duck Tails

During the mid- to late 1950s, a number of young people began to rebel against the clean-cut image of a well-scrubbed teenager with a crew cut and a bright smile. Jelly rolls and duck tails were the names of two hairstyles popular with some nonconformists, or rebels, during the late 1950s and early 1960s. Both required large amounts of hair oil or grease to shape the hair into the required style, therefore those who wore them were given the name greasers. Greasers were considered rebellious, dangerous, and a little vain, since their jelly rolls and duck tails required a lot of attention to keep them slick, smooth, and shaped correctly. They wore white T-shirts, straight-leg blue jeans, and black leather jackets, and they grew their hair long and slicked it back with various hair pomades (perfumed ointments), such as Brylcreem and Vaseline. For a jelly roll, boys combed their hair up and forward on the sides, to roll it together at the top of the head. This left a single large curl in the middle of the forehead. The duck tail, also called duck's ass or D.A., was created when both sides were combed together in the back of the head, then the tail of a comb was pulled down the center, creating a feathery look, which to some resembled the back end of a duck.

Various movie stars and rock 'n' roll musicians popularized the two greaser hairstyles, the most famous of which were actor James Dean (1931–1955) and musician Elvis Presley (1935–1977).

In the late 1950s Presley combed his hair into a softer, less greasy version of the jelly roll. Soon teenagers everywhere sported T-shirts, jeans, and greaser hair. Boys were not generally supposed to spend much time worrying about their looks, but a comb in the pocket became a necessary part of their wardrobe, since the jelly roll or D.A. required grooming throughout the day.

The new male obsession with hairstyle became the subject of many popular jokes of the time. The 1959 humorous hit song, "Kooky, Kooky, Lend Me Your Comb," by Ed Byrnes and Connie Stevens, was based on a duck-tailed private detective in the television series *77 Sunset Strip* (1958–64). One 1959 episode of the popular television show *Leave It to Beaver* (1957–63) was titled "Wally's Hair Comb" and involved a teenager and his parents' response to a jelly roll fad at school.

FOR MORE INFORMATION

Salamone, Frank. *Popular Culture in the Fifties.* Lanham, MD: University Press of America, 2001.

In the late 1950s singer Elvis Presley combed his hair into a softer, less greasy version of the jelly roll. *Reproduced by permission of AP/Wide World Photos.*

Pillbox Hats

Pillboxes are small containers used to hold pills. Beginning in the 1930s the basic pillbox design was employed by milliners, or hatmakers, who created a new style of head covering: the pillbox hat, a smallish, brimless round hat that featured straight sides and a level top. Pillbox hats were popular because of their simplicity and elegance. They most often came in solid colors and were usually unadorned with accessories except for a colored net veil, or a single pin or jewel. They were, however, made of an array of materials, some of which were elaborately designed. These included green wool with

Woman wearing pink pillbox hat. With its simple-yet-elegant design, the pillbox hat could be worn unadorned or accessorized. *Reproduced by permission of © Bettmann/CORBIS.*

ornate gold cording; black velvet, smothered in black beads; and white organdy, a transparent fabric, with attached overlapping organdy petals and silk rose bouquets. Pillbox hats might also be made out of the furs of mink, lynx, fox, or leopard skin. Musician Bob Dylan (1941–) incorporated the image of the latter into a song about a jilted lover, "Leopard-Skin Pillbox Hat" (1966).

The popularity of the pillbox hat increased during the post–World War II (1939–45) era and reached its peak at the 1961 inauguration of President John F. Kennedy (1917–1963), when his wife, Jacqueline Kennedy (1929–1994), wore a simple, unadorned bone wool pillbox hat designed by Halston (1932–1990). Previously, Mrs. Kennedy did not favor hats of any kind, but she was so taken by Halston's design that the pillbox hat became her trademark. She even was wearing a pink one on November 22, 1963, as she cradled her husband in her arms moments after he was shot while riding in a Dallas, Texas, motorcade. The cheerful femininity of Jackie Kennedy's pink suit and pillbox hat are ironic reminders of that tragic day.

FOR MORE INFORMATION

Garland-Dewson, Ruth. *Hats for Every Head: The Language of Hats.* Fort Bragg, CA: Cypress House, 2003.

McDowell, Colin. *Hats: Status, Style, and Glamour.* New York: Rizzoli, 1992.

Probert, Christine, ed. *Hats in Vogue Since 1910.* New York: Abbeville Press, 1982.

Body Decorations, 1946–60

Proper accessories, makeup, and undergarments were an extremely important part of women's fashion in the late 1940s through the 1950s. The major fashion trends of the late 1940s, inspired by the New Look fashions of designer Christian Dior (1905–1957), called for a carefully assembled outfit that included such accessories as white gloves and umbrellas to accompany carefully chosen shoes, hat, and dress. The New Look called for tasteful but understated jewelry. One of the most important accessories was the handbag, or purse. Most women would not go out without a handbag. According to a *New York Times* article from 1945: "A woman without her handbag feels as lost as a wanderer in the desert."

There were other items that a well-dressed woman considered indispensable. Makeup, for example, was very important to the well-put-together ensemble. Numerous manufacturers offered makeup to women, and makeup advertising accounted for 11 percent of all advertising by 1950. Nail polish on the toenails became an important part of a woman's collection, especially after the mass production of plastic shoes which revealed the toes began in the late 1940s. As with all other items of a wardrobe, nail polish and makeup were chosen so that the colors complemented the outfit. When tight sweaters came into style in the mid-1950s, there was a short-lived craze for what is known as a "sweater girl" bra. This bra shaped a woman's breasts into stiff, pointed cones. The look was popularized by film star Jane Russell (1921–), as well as by several other busty 1950s screen stars. Young girls were especially fond of charm bracelets, which became trendy in the 1950s and continues in a lesser form to this day.

Men did not accessorize as much as women, but they did have several items they might wear to distinguish their outfits. A well-dressed man could choose from a range of cuff links, tie bars, and

CRISTÓBAL BALENCIAGA

Cristóbal Balenciaga (1895-1972), born in Guetaria, Spain, is one of the giants of twentieth-century fashion. His mother, a dressmaker, taught him needlework and dressmaking, and he apprenticed with tailors in Madrid and San Sebastian before opening his first dress shop in 1919. Balenciaga often journeyed to Paris, France, to observe the latest designs and purchase dresses for his shop. In 1936 he opened the House of Balenciaga in Paris. Here Balenciaga created haute couture, or high fashion, a phrase that pertains to ground-breaking clothing styles originated by designers and meant to be worn by the famous and wealthy.

Almost immediately Balenciaga won a sizeable American clientele. His popularity expanded after the end of World War II (1939–45), when the world again became style-conscious. Queens, princesses, duchesses, movie stars, and the wives of millionaires often were photographed for the pages of newspaper society columns and fashion magazines wearing the latest Balenciaga creation.

Balenciaga believed that the body and the clothing that covered it needed to coexist in harmony. In his dress designs he was determined that the cut of the material adhered to the shape of the body, and his designs generally did not radically alter from season to season. His daytime clothing was straightforward yet stylish: a simple black wool dress, for example, or a beige sleeveless blouse and charcoal gray two-piece suit with leather belt. His evening wear was more extravagant and playful, with his designs employing abundantly decorated fabrics, heavy beading, protruding shoulders, and broad, full skirts. A characteristic Balenciaga evening dress might be floor-length and strapless, trimmed in white floral lace on a black net base. It was worn over a gray silk taffeta petticoat, and came with a pink silk taffeta cummerbund, or waistband.

Quite a few of Balenciaga's designs were based on regional Spanish clothing. He employed the vivid colors of the Spanish countryside and was inspired by the outfits worn by flamenco dancers and bullfighters and the lengthy blouses and boots worn by Basque fishermen in northern Spain. He also was influenced by the art of the master Spanish artists, particularly Francisco Goya (1746–1828). It often was said that Balenciaga employed color in a manner similar to the way in which painters use paint to bring life to their subjects.

Balenciaga believed that a tastefully designed outfit needed to be topped off with the essence of a delicate perfume. With this in mind he marketed his initial fragrance in 1947, which he named Le Dix. Subsequent Balenciaga perfumes were called Rumba, Talisman, Quadrille, and, appropriately, Cristóbal.

Unlike later celebrity designers who were bent on self-promotion and became stars in their own right, Balenciaga remained aloof from the public. He was not known to mingle with his clients, and he regularly observed the introduction of his latest collection while perched behind a white curtain. He allowed himself to be known only to a fortunate few, which added to his mystique. Balenciaga designed his last collection in 1968 and died four years later.

collar pins, made in gold, silver, or a new metal called palladium. Wristwatches continued to be popular among men. A new wristwatch called a Timex was introduced in 1950 with an advertising campaign that boasted that the Timex could "take a licking and keep on ticking." By the late 1950s one in every three watches sold in the United States was a Timex.

FOR MORE INFORMATION

Daniel, Anita. "Inside Story of a Handbag." *New York Times* (January 21, 1945).

Ewing, Elizabeth. *History of Twentieth Century Fashion.* Revised by Alice Mackrell. Lanham, MD: Barnes and Noble Books, 1992.

Jouve, Marie-Andrée. *Balenciaga.* New York: Rizzoli, 1980.

Miller, Lesley Ellis. *Cristóbal Balenciaga (Fashion Designers Series).* New York: Holmes and Meier Publishers, 1993.

Schoeffler, O. E., and William Gale. *Esquire's Encyclopedia of 20th Century Men's Fashions.* New York: McGraw-Hill, 1973.

Steele, Valerie. *Fifty Years of Fashion: New Look to Now.* New Haven, CT: Yale University Press, 1997.

Charm Bracelet

Charm bracelets actually date from ancient times. They were worn by men as well as women and were intended to protect one from one's adversaries or reflect one's profession, religious or political affiliation, or status within the community. They came in a range of styles. Chinese bracelets, for example, included jade carvings, metal objects, and glass beads, all of which were attached to a black string and fastened to the wrist. Originally charm bracelets were meant to have a magical effect on the wearer, but the bracelet's purpose and meaning and evolution into a fashion statement changed with the shifting culture and values of the twentieth century.

The typical twentieth-century charm bracelet was adorned with objects representing good luck (a four-leaf clover, horseshoe, or dice), happiness (an elephant), prosperity (a pig), or dreams coming true (a wishbone). Love, represented by a heart, was a favored theme. Variations included obsessive love or infatuation (a heart pierced by an arrow), love put forth and returned (two hearts pierced by one arrow), and devotion to the one you love (a padlocked heart).

A cheerleader megaphone, telephone, cat, dog, or money bag represented items the wearer desired or already had possessed or achieved.

More expensive charm bracelets were made of silver or gold, while less costly ones were stainless steel, copper, or brass. Their charms often came in a variety of materials; small plastic ones were even purchased in gumball machines or came as prizes in candy boxes. A girl's charm bracelet eventually was replaced by a wedding band, at which point the bracelet was retired to a jewelry box as a keepsake of her youth. Some grown women, however, also wore charm bracelets.

FOR MORE INFORMATION

Congram, Marjorie. *Charms to Collect*. Martinsville, NJ: Dockwra Press, 1988.

Oldford, Kathleen. *My Mother's Charms: Timeless Gifts of Family Wisdom*. San Francisco, CA: HarperSanFrancisco, 2001.

[*See also* **Volume 4, 1930–45: Charm Bracelet**]

Makeup

During World War II (1939–45) so many chemicals and other resources were used for the war effort that cosmetics had become scarce and expensive. After the war the market was once again flooded with products, and women were encouraged to shop and buy in order to keep the economy healthy. In addition, many women who had filled jobs left open when men had gone to war had adopted a more practical and masculine way of dressing. Government leaders wanted these women to give their jobs back to men returning from the military, and so leaders stressed a return to feminine roles, such as wife and mother. Fashion designers too, emphasized a return to femininity, such as the New Look created by French designer Christian Dior (1905–1957), which featured lavish designs with full skirts and tight waists that showed womanly curves.

The look for women of the late 1940s and early 1950s was very showy and decorative, and it required makeup. Lipstick, liquid or cream makeup base, powder, rouge, eye shadow, eyeliner, mascara, and fingernail polish became a part of most women's daily routine, and many women said they felt naked until they had "put their face on." By 1950 11 percent of all advertising in the United States was for cosmetics, according to Dorothy and Thomas Hoobler's *Vanity Rules*. New companies formed to make and sell beauty products. Esteé Lauder manufactured very expensive cosmetics, and women bought them, assuming that the high price tag promised especially good quality. Hazel Bishop made affordable cosmetics for working women who could not spend a lot on makeup and sold them at discount stores, where working-class women shopped. Johnson Products, founded by George Johnson in 1954, sold beauty products designed specifically for African American women's skin and hair. From this point on cosmetics were a major industry in the West.

Actress Grace Kelly wearing 1950s-style makeup. The new beauty products of the 1950s ushered in an era in which the well-dressed woman was expected to wear makeup. *Reproduced by permission of © CinemaPhoto/CORBIS.*

FOR MORE INFORMATION

Hoobler, Dorothy, and Thomas Hoobler. *Vanity Rules: A History of American Fashion and Beauty.* Brookfield, CT: Twenty-First Century Books, 2000.

Peiss, Kathy Lee. *Hope in a Jar: The Making of America's Beauty Culture.* New York: Metropolitan Books, 1998.

[*See also* **Volume 4, 1900–18: Lipstick; Volume 4, 1919–29: Makeup**]

Footwear, 1946–60

Men's shoes did not go through a great deal of change in the fifteen years following the end of World War II (1939–45). During the late 1940s, while Bold Look, or showy, fashions were in style, there was a brief preference for thicker-soled, heavier shoes to accompany the bolder cuts and colors in men's suits. By the 1950s, however, as suit styles became more conservative, men turned to lighter soled, traditionally cut dress shoe styles such as moccasins, wing tips, or bluchers, heavy, blunt-toed oxfords. For casual wear, men could turn to the newly popular Top-Sider, a comfortable moccasin-style shoe with a no-slip sole. Late in the 1950s Italian shoe styles became popular. These were longer and lighter in weight, with a low-cut upper. Finally, for children, young adults, and active adults, the tennis shoe or athletic shoe remained the shoe of choice.

Women's shoe styles, like women's fashion in general, were much more vibrant. The New Look fashions that took the world by storm in the late 1940s brought a renewed concern for style and elegance in shoes. The shoes that were chosen with New Look outfits had pointed toes and revealed more of the foot than earlier shoes. Over the years the heel in women's dress shoes grew slimmer and slimmer. In the early 1950s the stiletto heel, which came to a nearly needle-like point, saw this trend reach its peak. As hemlines in women's dresses rose late in the 1950s, heels actually became shorter and less pointed. The standard women's shoe was the pump, offered in an array of cuts and colors to mix and match with other outfits. Finally, the emergence of new technologies during this period allowed for the invention of plastic shoes in 1947. Within a few years plastic shoes were made in a variety of colors and styles.

FOR MORE INFORMATION

Ewing, Elizabeth. *History of Twentieth Century Fashion.* Revised by Alice Mackrell. Lanham, MD: Barnes and Noble Books, 1992.

Schoeffler, O. E., and William Gale. *Esquire's Encyclopedia of 20th Century Men's Fashions.* New York: McGraw-Hill, 1973.

Steele, Valerie. *Fifty Years of Fashion: New Look to Now.* New Haven, CT: Yale University Press, 1997.

Plastic Shoes

Man-made materials invented in the 1940s created a new chapter in fashion history by replacing natural textiles, such as leather and cotton, in many fashionable garments. The new materials were advertised as "miracles" because of how easy they were to care for: no shrinking, no staining, and no need for ironing. Plastic shoes were among the most popular clothing items made from these new materials. They were shiny and vibrantly colored, or even clear. The newness of plastic combined with its easy care and waterproof qualities made plastic shoes a favorite form of footwear.

Plastic shoes were mainly formed as sandals. Early women's styles included sandals with wooden wedge-shaped soles and plastic straps. A popular style called the Peek-a-boo featured a wide plastic strap over the front of the foot with a small opening at the front to show some of the woman's toes. Children's styles were sandals made entirely of plastic and either fastened with buckles or snaps. Plastic shoes' brilliant colors triggered another fashion fad. As part of a trend toward coordinating outfits that was part of the American Look, women began painting their fingernails and toenails the same bright colors as their plastic shoes.

Even though plastic shoes do not breathe, or let air in to cool off or vent, leaving feet hot and sweaty, their popularity continues to the present day. By the 1980s both children and women wore soft plastic sandals called jellies. Taiwan exported 520 million pairs of plastic shoes in 1983, nearly enough for one out of every nine people on the planet. Plastic flip-flops and plastic shoes remained popular into the twenty-first century, with some designer sandals costing more than one hundred dollars a pair.

FOR MORE INFORMATION

Cosgrave, Bronwyn. *The Complete History of Costume and Fashion from Ancient Egypt to the Present Day*. New York: Checkmark Books, 2000.

Stiletto Heel

Women have worn high-heeled shoes for hundreds of years, but the heel has never been so tall and narrow as on the stiletto heels that became popular in the early 1950s. A stiletto heel, named after a thin Italian dagger, could be as tall as four or five inches, and it narrowed to a point as small as three-eighths of an inch in diameter. The shoes forced women to stand on their tiptoes, clench their calf muscles, and thrust their chest forward for balance. The dramatic stance that the heels forced women to adopt was said to make the wearer look sexy and glamorous.

A pair of platform stiletto-heeled shoes. First developed in the 1950s, the stiletto was a menace to women's bodies and the surfaces on which they walked. *Reproduced by permission of AP/Wide World Photos.*

Italian designer Roger Vivier (1913–1998) invented the stiletto to accompany clothes designed by French fashion designer Christian Dior (1905–1957) in the early 1950s. The stiletto, like other fashions of the time, was not at all practical. It highlighted women's femininity, but the shoe was also a hazard to women's bodies and to the surfaces they walked on. Podiatrists, or doctors who treat the feet, warned that the shoes caused harm to the tendon, bone deformities, and back pain. The pointy heels tore carpets and scarred solid flooring; by the late 1950s airlines and some buildings had actually banned the heels.

Despite their dangers, stiletto heels remained popular throughout the late 1950s and early 1960s and staged a comeback in the 1990s. Popular 1950s actress Jayne Mansfield (1932–1967) claimed to have two hundred pairs of the heels, and actress Elizabeth Taylor (1932–) received notoriety for the scene in the movie *Butterfield 8* (1960) in which she digs her stiletto heel into a man's shoe. In the film *Single White Female* (1992) actress Jennifer Jason Leigh's (1962–) character took the danger of the stiletto a step further when she used the steel spike of her stiletto heel to kill a man. Stiletto heels remain to some a potent symbol of female power and sexuality.

FOR MORE INFORMATION

Ewing, Elizabeth. *History of Twentieth Century Fashion.* Revised by Alice Mackrell. Lanham, MD: Barnes and Noble Books, 1992.

[*See also* **Volume 4, 1919–29: High-Heeled Shoes**]

Top-Siders

Top-Siders, also known as boat shoes or deck shoes, are casual low-heeled shoes made out of leather or canvas with a special skid-resistant sole, usually made out of white rubber. The shoes became popular in the late 1940s, following the end of restrictions on the use of leather and rubber that were associated with World War II (1939–45). They were first popular with the "boating set," upper-class easterners who spent their leisure time sailing yachts that often had slippery decks and who needed the shoes' nonskid soles. The shoes were later associated with the preppy look of the 1950s, which was revived by designer Ralph Lauren (1939–) in the 1980s.

The upscale image associated with the Top-Sider was not what was intended by their inventor, Paul Sperry (1894–1982). A devoted sailor, Sperry one day noticed that his cocker spaniel, Prince, had much better traction on a slippery boat deck than he did. Examining the dog's paws, Sperry observed a crisscrossing web of cracks and splits. Sperry began experimenting by making razor cuts in the surface of a slab of gum rubber that he used as a shoe sole.

By 1935 he had created a herringbone (a weave that creates rows of parallel lines sloping in opposite directions) pattern of cuts that reduced slipping dramatically. He worked with the Converse Rubber Company, a tennis shoe manufacturer, to produce the soles and then mount them to a leather moccasin-style top to create the Sperry Top-Sider.

Sperry Top-Siders were soon widely imitated, with many manufacturers producing a variant boat shoe. In 2003 the original Sperry Top-Sider, called the Authentic Original, continued to be made exactly as the first version.

FOR MORE INFORMATION

"Top-Sider Creation." *Sperry Top-Sider: Where Performance Counts.* http://www.sperrytopsider.com/creation.asp (accessed on August 27, 2003).

Troubled Times: 1961–79

The 1960s and 1970s were decades of real contrast in the West. While the global political situation was actually stabilized by the tensions of the Cold War (1945–91), both the United States and European countries experienced internal political turmoil, including assassinations of major political leaders, protests, and widespread movements for social change. Economies boomed across the West during the 1960s, but the citizens of these countries were not necessarily content with their widespread prosperity. Then, in the 1970s, economic growth stalled and people focused more on personal issues than political problems. Unfazed by these political and economic shifts, the United States continued as the world's greatest producer and consumer of entertainment. Musicians, movie stars, and television stars gained unusual influence in shaping popular culture.

Vietnam and Cold Wars

Relations between countries were given real stability in the 1960s and 1970s by the ongoing conflict between the United States and the Soviet Union known as the Cold War. In this conflict, nations across the globe either allied themselves and their political and economic system with the capitalist United States, where people had the opportunity to seek out economic gain for themselves, or the Communist Soviet Union, where individuals could not own property, and the profits of everyone's labor were pooled and distributed by the government, which was controlled by the Communist Party. (A third option was neutrality, though few nations chose this path.) Western Europe and the Americas sided with the United States, while Eastern Europe, China, and parts of Asia followed the lead of the Soviet Union. Though there were very tense moments between the two sides—an American U2 spy plane was shot down over the Soviet Union in 1960, the Soviets placed missiles in Cuba in 1962, and the Soviets invaded Afghanistan in 1979—for the most part the Cold War was a war of words and military buildup, with both nations committing vast amounts of money to building weapons instead of using them on each other.

Bloody conflicts did break out during this period, however. A civil war in the Southeast Asian nation of Vietnam pitted the Communist northern part of the nation, backed by the Soviets and China, against the capitalist southern portion, backed by the French and later the United States. The Vietnam War (1954–75) devastated the country itself and also proved very costly for the United States and the Soviet Union, which provided money and soldiers. The war was very controversial in the United States. Many people felt that the United States shouldn't be so involved in another country's war. They staged mass protests that caused President Lyndon B. Johnson (1908–1973) not to run for re-election in 1968.

Movements for social change

The protest against the Vietnam War was one of many protest movements that characterized political life in the West during the 1960s and 1970s. Two of the biggest movements were the Civil Rights movement and the Women's Liberation movement. The Civil Rights movement, led by Martin Luther King Jr. (1929–1968), Malcolm X (1925–1965), and a range of other activists, was a sustained effort to end racial discrimination in the United States. The movement, which staged bus boycotts and marches to force change, was active throughout the 1960s, and many of its goals were achieved by the time King was assassinated in 1968. Inspired by the struggle to gain civil rights for African Americans, the Women's Liberation movement was a loosely organized effort to secure equal rights for women. This international movement, which was most visible in the 1970s, helped improve women's prospects in the workplace and ended many laws that discriminated against women.

The power of youth

These movements and several others, including movements for homosexual rights and environmental awareness, shared one thing: the intense involvement of people in their teens and twenties. Young people became increasingly active politically across the West in the 1960s. They demanded that their voices be heard in political matters, and they began to exert a real influence on popular culture. Nowhere was the influence of youth felt more than in the area of fashion and clothing. Beginning in the 1960s, young people began to reject the clothes offered to them by the fashion industry and to invent new clothing styles of their own. From the mods and the rockers of early 1960s London, England, to the hippie dropouts of the United States in the late 1960s, to the punks and disco dancers of the 1970s, young people defined the styles that were then taken up throughout the world. Similar kinds of youth influence were felt in the areas of music, television, and film, as rock bands, actors, and actresses were lifted to celebrity status thanks to the support of young people.

Young people were somewhat troubled by a growing phenomenon in Western cultures: the growth of consumerism, which meant that people had enough money to allow them to produce a range of goods beyond the bare necessities. Western countries in general, and the United States in particular, enjoyed immense prosperity during the 1960s. People had more disposable income (income that was not needed for food and shelter) than ever before in history, and they used that money to buy televisions, automobiles, clothes, and other consumer items. Corporations became very skilled at mass-producing items for sale around the world. Even when economies declined in the 1970s, consumerism remained a major force in the West.

Young people worried that the great wealth produced in the West could be better spent on combating issues such as poverty and crime. They didn't want to purchase just for the sake of purchasing. They wanted the things they bought and wore to reflect their values and ideals. Companies, including clothing companies, constantly sought to change their products in order to satisfy the desires of these consumers. In fashion this shifting consumer demand, rather than the creations of designers, drove what was offered. The most successful designers learned to give the people what they wanted, which during the 1960s and 1970s was variety and comfort.

Most of the major social and political changes of this period had an effect on the fashions people wore. People throughout the West were becoming more aware of the need to respect different cultural traditions and to allow for individual differences. In the 1960s this led to fads favoring the fashions of Native Americans, African Americans, and other cultures of the world. By the 1970s tastes in clothing had become even more individualized. It was said that people could wear anything they wanted—and did. Women especially were tired of having fashions dictated to them, and they chose clothes that were comfortable and liberating. This focus on

HALSTON

In terms of fashion, the 1970s was the decade of the American designer Halston (1932–1990). His designs were simple but elegant, and he favored flawlessly tailored classic cuts. His clothes could be worn year-round, during the day and evening. His dress designs eventually became so minimal that they even came without zippers and buttons. Halston's greatest fame came from his reputation as the designer of choice for celebrities. His clients included Elizabeth Taylor (1932–), Liza Minnelli (1946–), Andy Warhol (c. 1928–1987), Anjelica Huston (1951–), Bianca Jagger (1950–), Martha Graham (1894–1991), Barbara Walters (1931–), and first lady Jacqueline Kennedy Onassis (1929–1994). He once observed, "You're only as good as the people you dress," according to his biographers Elaine Gross and Fred Rottman.

Born Roy Halston Frowick in Des Moines, Iowa, he enjoyed sewing and making hats as a child. After briefly attending Indiana University and the Chicago Art Institute, he worked as a window dresser while designing hats on the side. He also decided to take his middle name as his profes-

sional name. His hat designs soon proved popular, and in 1957 he opened his own store in Chicago, Illinois. Two years later he settled in New York and was employed as a hat designer at Bergdorf Goodman, a fashionable department store. He soon became nationally famous by designing the bone wool pillbox hat that Jacqueline Kennedy, the incoming first lady, wore at the 1961 inauguration of her husband, John F. Kennedy (1917–1963). At the time the hats worn by women on formal occasions were intricately designed and featured an assortment of added-on items like fur, feathers, and even jewelry. Halston's pillbox was just the opposite; it was a straightforward, unadorned, minimal design. Its popularity helped to usher in shorter, simpler hairstyles for women.

In 1966 Halston created Bergdorf's first ready-to-wear collection. (Ready-to-wear refers to clothes can be worn right off the rack versus custom-made designs.) Two years later he launched his own fashion salon. His career peaked during the following decade and the Halston name was licensed to a range of products, including sheets, shoes, and an especially lucrative series of fragrances. He marketed a synthetic, or man-made, fabric that he called Ultrasuede: a supersoft, su-

individual tastes and expression helped earn the 1970s the nickname the "Me Decade."

FOR MORE INFORMATION

Bluttal, Steven, ed. Essays by Patricia Mears. *Halston.* London, England: Phaidon Press, 2001.

Feinstein, Stephen. *The 1960s: From the Vietnam War to Flower Power.* Berkeley Heights, NJ: Enslow Publishers, 2000.

Feinstein, Stephen. *The 1970s: From Watergate to Disco.* Berkeley Heights, NJ: Enslow Publishers, 2000.

Gross, Elaine, and Fred Rottman. *Halston: An American Original.* New York: HarperCollins, 1999.

Holland, Gini. *The 1960s.* San Diego, CA: Lucent Books, 1999.

perfine material that had the look and feel of real suede but was far more durable. Ultrasuede was his fabric of choice for another of his innovations: the shirtdress, a dress designed to look like a shirt, complete with collar and buttons.

Before Halston, fashion shows were trade events that primarily catered to buyers from retail store chains. Halston had the idea to transform them into glittery extravaganzas, complete with flashing lights and popular music. Thanks to Halston's influence, the fashion show became a performance, similar to a rock concert or a big budget stage show.

Halston's celebrity clients also became his close friends. He was a regular at the most stylish New York parties and nightspots, usually dressed in a black cashmere turtleneck. However, Halston's power in the fashion industry began to wane in the late 1970s. He was unable to keep up with the constant demand for new designs, and he made a critical mistake by allowing his Halston label clothes to be sold at the middle-class retail chain J. C. Penney. This business decision drove away the celebrity consumers who once liked his exclusive clothes. Halston died of AIDS (acquired immune deficiency syndrome) in 1990.

Halston, left, created designs that were simple but elegant.
Reproduced by permission of © Bettmann/CORBIS.

Layman, Richard, ed. *American Decades: 1960–1969.* Detroit, MI: Gale Research, 1995.

Layman, Richard, ed. *American Decades: 1970–1979.* Detroit, MI: Gale Research, 1995.

Stewart, Gail. *The 1970s.* San Diego, CA: Lucent Books, 1999.

Clothing, 1961–79

In fashion, the 1960s and the 1970s were decades of repeated revolutionary change. The youth explosion and mod craze of the early 1960s were followed quickly by the hippie look of the late 1960s, the antifashion trends of the early 1970s, and the punk and disco styles of the mid- to late 1970s. By the late 1970s, people throughout the West seemed content to wear "regular" clothes once more. Taken together, these high profile fashion fads forever changed the way the fashion industry worked.

Before the 1960s high-profile designers in Paris, France, and London, England, in cooperation with celebrity fashion trendsetters, had dictated the styles that were worn by people of all ages. Under this fashion system, news about what was stylish to wear came from the top down. Designers created a line of clothing, rich people bought the originals, and clothing retailers sold copies to the common man and woman. During and after the 1960s, common people, especially young people, began to exercise far more control in determining what was in style, and designers increasingly tried to keep up with the newest trends. Under the new fashion system, new styles were invented by people in hot cultural scenes or by rock bands; followers adopted and modified the new styles; and designers then copied the new styles and marketed them to the masses through a growing assortment of retail outlets.

Rebellious young people known as mods and rockers began to invent their own clothing in trendy parts of London. Women wore very short skirts, tall, brightly colored boots, and clinging, sleeveless tunics. Young men wore suits in bright paisley patterns, boxy jackets, and high-topped, black leather boots, or they wore leather jackets and shirts made of British flags, like rock star Pete Townshend (1945–) of the rock band the Who. The boldly colored new styles worn by men took a name of their own, the Peacock Revolution, and were striking because men's styles before this time were so conservative.

Vogue magazine, the world's premier source for fashion information, called this fashion upsurge "Youthquake." The fashion movement was led by young people, such as British designer Mary Quant (1934–), who shares credit with French designer André Courreges (1923–) for the introduction of the one garment most associated with the youth explosion: the miniskirt. Quant famously

Trendsetters in 1970 London. The bold, new fashions of the Peacock Revolution were a far cry from traditional men's styles.
Reproduced by permission of AP/Wide World Photos.

denied that she had created the miniskirt, claiming that it was the "girls in the street who did it." Her point was that the new styles were created by young people who rejected the old-fashioned system and created clothes that expressed their own values. These young people often followed the lead of rock stars like the members of the bands the Beatles, the Who, and the Rolling Stones who were notorious for rejecting existing styles and creating new ones.

Hippies

The various London-based youth fashion fads dominated clothing trends through the mid-1960s, but soon a new trend took its place. Emerging first on the West Coast of the United States, the hippies were one of the most colorful and high-profile social movements of an interesting decade. Hippies rejected their parents' values about sex, work, and patriotism. They protested against the U.S. war in Vietnam (1954–75), switched sexual partners freely, experimented with drugs, and "dropped out" of regular society. They wanted clothes that reflected their values and adopted a huge range of diverse styles, from fringe looks that paid respect to Native Americans, to various exotic fashions borrowed from Indian, Asian, and other cultures, to hand-me-down and thrift store clothes that showed their rejection of materialism. Though hippie styles are usually associated with long hair, tie-dyed shirts, long skirts for women, jeans for men, and paisley and flowered patterns, in truth hippie styles were extremely varied.

The choices hippies made about clothing were a direct criticism of fashion, the system by which certain elite designers and trendsetters determine what everyone wears. Hippies wanted everyone to choose for themselves. Even though they tried to be antifashion, the fashion industry celebrated and borrowed from hippie clothing, making such things as the long wrap dress, the fringed shirt, blue jeans, and other items available to the masses. But in doing so the fashion industry recognized that its control was over.

Diverse styles

By the early 1970s clothing styles had gone off in so many different directions that it was difficult for anyone to say what was in fashion and what was not. Men and women had a great variety of

MOD STYLES AND THE LONDON SCENE

In the early to mid-1960s, London, England, briefly became the fashion center of the world as a revolution in style rocked the world of dress. Carnaby Street was a street in the Soho section of London that was home to many of the innovative boutiques and shops associated with London fashion of the mid-1960s. The most famous of these was His Clothes, the flagship of a chain opened in 1957 by clothier John Stephen, whose outrageous looks, cheap prices, and fast turnover of styles helped transform menswear fashion retailing. Stephen's mod, short for modern, designs and relaxed sales approach signaled a break with the stuffy customs of conventional British clothing shops, and helped turn Carnaby Street into a center for young clothes fanatics of both sexes.

The changes in men's fashions were labeled a "Peacock Revolution" by *Esquire* magazine columnist George Frazier (1911–1974), one of the first mainstream journalists to take notice of the flamboyant fashions parading along Carnaby Street. These fashions included Nehru jackets (close-fitted, single-breasted coats with stand-up collars and no lapels) in psychedelic colors and patterns, velvet suits, bold patterned shirts and ties, and pointy-toed boots with high heels. John Stephen dressed rock stars like the Who and the Rolling Stones, creating a unisex look marked by long, exquisitely styled hair and a lean silhouette, or shape. Their clothes were flamboyant and designed to attract attention. Even the Beatles traded in their drab gray suits for paisley scarves, flowered shirts, and striped bell-bottomed pants in the mid-1960s. Lines between the sexes became so blurred that a 1964 London *Sunday Times* magazine article on London styles famously asked "Is that a boy, or is it a girl?" Despite, or perhaps because of, this ambiguity, the look became extremely popular, even outside of Great Britain. The French designer Pierre Cardin (1922–) created an American version of the slim-lined European silhouette, which, along with the immense popularity of jeans, led to the acceptance of extremely close-fitting clothing.

The young women of London wore their hair long as well, usually straight, or cropped into the angular cuts made popular by hair stylist Vidal Sassoon (1928–). One of the great influences on women's fashions of this period was designer Mary Quant (1934–), who opened her flagship boutique Bazaar in 1958 on the Kings Road in London. Quant, who coined the word "youthquake" to describe what was going on in fashion at the time, sought to liberate women from the tyranny of the long skirt and cardigan with a series of fresh, innovative designs. These included a line of signature jumpers, ready-to-wear dresses, colored tights, hipster belts, plastic garments, sleeveless, crocheted tops, and her most celebrated

choices in what they wore. Men could still wear the standard business suit that looked much like it had in the 1950s, but they could also enliven their business look with brightly colored shirts, very wide neckties, or bell-bottom trousers. They could reject business attire altogether, wearing blue jeans and a T-shirt or even a jogging suit. Some women still discriminated between day wear and evening wear, but most women now chose from a range of dress styles depending on their personal preferences. Skirt lengths had changed so much, from the high-on-the-thigh mini to the knee-length midi to the ankle-length maxi, that anything was now permissible. And by

garment, the scandalously short miniskirt. The mini became a worldwide phenomenon, and Quant eventually branched out beyond clothes into cosmetics, all bearing her trademark five-petaled daisy.

Around 1967 the growth of the hippie movement and its styles replaced the London Scene as the center of fashion innovation, but in its brief period as a fashion center London had a huge influence on international styles.

Different Mary Quant mod styles. Her fashions, especially the miniskirt, were at the center of the 1960s "youthquake." *Reproduced by permission of AP/Wide World Photos.*

the 1970s pants were so common among women that they no longer attracted any comment.

One of the ways that people could stand out in such a tolerant clothing climate was to be deliberately bold or shocking. Hot pants (extremely short shorts), huge bell-bottoms, vividly colored leisure suits, polyester shirts, and tight catsuits are all examples of clothing styles that flirted with being over-the-top, but were fashionable for a time.

The two most distinct fashion fads of the 1970s grew out of very different music scenes. In the mid-1970s a subgenre of rock 'n' roll called punk rock—loud, fast, and angry—helped give birth to an entire punk scene, first in London and then in other major cities in the West. Punks wore ripped clothes, wildly spiked hairstyles, and huge Doc Marten boots, among other things. A very different style emerged from the disco scene, a dance-based music and culture trend that flourished in New York City in the mid-1970s. Disco dancers wore formal-looking clothes in flamboyant cuts and colors, including leisure suits and extremely skimpy dresses.

After nearly two decades of absolute excess, clothing styles became somewhat more conservative in the late 1970s. Aided by the rise of Italian fashion designers whose clothes were elegant and restrained, people in general turned to comfortable clothes that fit the body's natural contours. The end result of these tumultuous decades, however, was that most people felt completely free to assemble their wardrobe from a variety of clothes that best expressed their personal sense of style, rather than from a limited set of clothes determined by a selective fashion industry.

FOR MORE INFORMATION

Chenoune, Farid. *A History of Men's Fashion.* Paris, France: Flammarion, 1993.

Connikie, Yvonne. *Fashions of a Decade: The 1960s.* New York: Facts on File, 1990.

Contini, Mila. *Fashion: From Ancient Egypt to the Present Day.* Edited by James Laver. New York: Odyssey Press, 1965.

Cosgrave, Bronwyn. *The Complete History of Costume and Fashion: From Ancient Egypt to the Present Day.* New York: Checkmark Books, 2000.

Ewing, Elizabeth. *History of Twentieth Century Fashion.* Revised by Alice Mackrell. Lanham, MD: Barnes and Noble Books, 1992.

Herald, Jacqueline. *Fashions of a Decade: The 1970s.* New York: Facts on File, 1992.

Payne, Blanche, Geitel Winakor, and Jane Farrell-Beck. *The History of Costume.* 2nd ed. New York: HarperCollins, 1992.

Steele, Valerie. *Fifty Years of Fashion: New Look to Now.* New Haven, CT: Yale University Press, 1997.

A-line Skirt

A skirt that tapers gently out from a narrow waist, or a dress that grows gradually wider from the shoulder to the hem, is called an A-line, simply because its shape resembles the letter A. Though the tapered silhouette has been used during various fashion periods, it is generally agreed that the A-line dress became a staple of most women's wardrobes in the 1960s, just as styles were becoming simpler.

The modern A-line silhouette, or shape, was first seen during the mid-1950s, as part of French designer Christian Dior's (1905–1957) New Look. The New Look was a very feminine style, with sweeping skirts, tight tops that emphasized the bosom, and a narrow waist that emphasized full hips. Dior's styles especially emphasized full, tapered, A-shaped skirts, with the shape given by full underskirts. Despite the popularity of the New Look, it was not long before women sought a simpler style. Another French designer, Gabrielle "Coco" Chanel (1883–1971), who had become famous for simplifying fashion during the 1920s, introduced more body-hugging designs, and soon Dior had reduced the fullness of his skirts and introduced a simpler, smaller A-line dress.

This simple, geometric A-line dress fit in well with the modern look of the early 1960s, popular with women turning away from the fussy, frilly styles of the 1950s. The style was even more successful once it was worn by the new first lady of the United States, Jacqueline Kennedy (1929–94), who highly influenced fashion of the time. Women around the world admired the young first lady's sense of style and, once she began to wear the new A-line skirt, millions copied her. The A-line skirt has remained a classic style for decades.

FOR MORE INFORMATION

Cawthorne, Nigel. *The New Look: The Dior Revolution.* London, England: Reed Consumer Books, 1996.

Ewing, Elizabeth. *History of Twentieth Century Fashion.* Revised by Alice Mackrell. Lanham, MD: Barnes and Noble Books, 1992.

Steele, Valerie. *Fifty Years of Fashion: New Look to Now.* New Haven, CT: Yale University Press, 1997.

[*See also* Volume 5, 1946–60: New Look]

Bell-Bottoms

Bell-bottoms, pants with legs that become wider below the knee, were an extremely popular fashion during the 1960s and 1970s. The belled or flared legs on bell-bottom pants were originally a functional design, worn by those who worked on boats since the seventeenth century. The large legs allowed the pants to be easily rolled up out of the way for such messy jobs as washing the decks. In addition, if a sailor fell overboard, bell-bottom pants could be pulled off over boots or shoes and the wide legs inflated with air for use as a life preserver.

During the 1960s those who did not wish to conform to the strict, conservative clothing rules of the 1950s developed a new fashion. The clothing of this new fashion was inexpensive and extremely casual. Young people at the time rejected items from expensive clothing stores and shopped at secondhand stores and military surplus stores. Surplus navy bell-bottoms became one of the most popular items of dress. Wearing bits of old military uniforms had an added appeal for the largely antiwar counterculture youth of the late 1960s and early 1970s (those who were not in favor of the United States's involvement in the Vietnam War [1954–75]). Flowers embroidered on an old army jacket and colorful peace symbols applied to worn and faded navy bell-bottoms made a very personal antiwar statement. Bell-bottoms also fit in with the new unisex style, as both men and women wore them.

At first, viewing the new fashion as the dress of dangerous radicals, clothing manufacturers did not sell bell-bottoms. Those who could not find them at a local surplus store often made their straight leg jeans into fashionable bells by cutting the outside leg seam and sewing in a triangle of fabric to widen the leg. By the 1970s, however, designers had begun to market trendy bell-bottoms made out of a wide variety of materials. Entertainers from husband and wife team Sonny (1935–1998) and Cher (1946–) to singers James Brown (c. 1928–) and Pat Boone (1934–) wore "bells," which were often worn skin tight to the knee, then flared out in a wide, soft drape. Some pants were so wide that they were nicknamed "elephant bells."

Bell-bottoms, both wide and just slightly flared, made from denim, bright cotton, and satin polyester, were so popular that they

HIPPIES

A number of middle-class young people growing up in the late 1950s felt that they did not fit into accepted society. Not only did their futures seem planned out for them, with office jobs for the men and motherhood and housework for the women, but those futures also seemed boring and suffocating. In addition, there was an expanding war in Vietnam, and young men were being drafted into the army. By the late 1960s young people who wanted peace and personal freedom began to gather together to express their views. In 1967 people gathered at events like New York's Central Park Be-In and San Francisco's Summer of Love. In October 1967 over fifty thousand hippies gathered in Washington, D.C., to make a statement against the war by trying to levitate the Pentagon building, headquarters of the U.S. Department of Defense, with their collective mind power.

Hippies bonded around their antiwar feelings, but they also broke away from the restrictions of society by practicing "free love" or casual sex, and using drugs, especially marijuana and the hallucinatory drug LSD, both for fun and to open their minds to new ways of seeing the world. Hippies, or freaks, as they often called themselves, also connected around the music of the time, a mixture of protest folk and rock. The 1969 Woodstock Festival and Concert was an important event in hippie culture. Planned for an audience of 150,000, the rock festival in upstate New York attracted 500,000 fans and was a celebration of love, peace, and music.

Hippie style included long, flowing hair for both men and women, and often beards for men. Since hippies rejected the modern American mainstream, ethnic clothes were popular, as were old-fashioned styles. Both men and women commonly wore headbands, floppy hats, flowing scarves, and beads with blue jeans or bell-bottoms and tie-dyed T-shirts. Rebelling against corporate culture meant making clothes or buying cheaply at thrift shops and military surplus stores, so clothes were often ragged and patched or embroidered. Flowered clothing and embroidery were popular, and flowers became an important hippie symbol because hippies revered and felt connected to nature. "Flower power" was a term used to describe the hippie movement, and it was not uncommon for hippies at antiwar demonstrations to give flowers to police and soldiers, even placing flowers in the muzzles of their guns.

Though the hippies grew older and styles changed, people continued to feel nostalgic about hippie style and values. The 1980s and 1990s saw occasional revivals of hippie fashions and music, if not hippie values.

became a symbol of the outlandish and colorful style of the 1970s, and when the decade ended many hoped that bell-bottoms were gone for good. Like many of the items of clothing strongly identified with the 1970s, bell-bottoms became a symbol of old-fashioned bad taste. However, the flared pants returned to style in the 1990s as part of a trend toward baggy clothing.

FOR MORE INFORMATION

Dustan, Keith. *Just Jeans: The Story 1970–1995.* Kew, Victoria: Australian Scholarly Press, 1995.

Catsuit

Formfitting stretch body suits known as catsuits were the ultimate in slinky style and casual comfort for women during the 1960s. The all-in-one garment was typically either zipped or buttoned at the front, from the navel to the neck, and was often worn

The catsuit combined the leotard's functionality with futuristic style.
Reproduced by permission of AP/Wide World Photos.

with boots. Catsuits first took off in 1964 when the French designer André Courreges (1923–) introduced his Space Age collection. Intended to capture the public imagination inspired by the space program, Courreges' designs included futuristic plastic goggles, silver moon boots, and astronaut helmets. But the centerpiece of his women's line was the knitted, long-sleeved, one-piece catsuit. Made out of synthetic, or manmade, material and so named because of its slinky fit, it became one of the signature women's garments of the 1960s. Other designers, most notably Pierre Cardin (1922–), also began creating bodysuits that drew on Courreges' futuristic design.

Comic book heroes Superman and Batman had worn variations on the catsuit for years, of course, so it was no great leap when female superheroines began turning up in them. In the United States the television series *Batman* provided a weekly forum for catsuit style, beginning in 1967. Catwoman and Batgirl each sported patent leather bodysuits designed to emphasize the power and confidence of the newly liberated female. But perhaps the most famous catsuit wearer of all was the British TV superheroine Emma Peel of the series *The Avengers* (1961–69). As portrayed by actress Diana Rigg (1938–), Mrs. Peel epitomized the swinging 1960s vixen in her cutout black leather catsuit, created for her by the program's costumers John Bates and Alun Hughes. After Rigg wore a wetsuit-type catsuit on the show, designers everywhere copied the sleek look.

Catsuits fell out of favor in the 1970s with the return of more natural fabrics. The look briefly returned in the 1990s, as rappers like Missy Elliott and Dee-Lite's Lady Miss Kier brought back the catsuit in psychedelic patterns, often paired with platform shoes.

FOR MORE INFORMATION

Connikie, Yvonne. *Fashions of a Decade: The 1960s.* New York: Facts on File, 1990.

Powe-Temperley, Kitty. *20th Century Fashions: The 60s.* Milwaukee, WI: Gareth Stevens Publishing, 1999.

A model wearing a hip-hugging corduroy skirt at a 1966 fashion show. First popular during the 1700s, corduroy was again trendy during the 1960s and 1970s. *Reproduced by permission of AP/Wide World Photos.*

Corduroy

Sometimes called the "poor man's velvet," corduroy is a soft, durable fabric that has been popular among people of all classes for almost two centuries. Usually made of cotton or cotton blended with such man-made fabrics as rayon and polyester, corduroy is woven with loose threads that are then cut to create a pile, or thick, soft texture. Most corduroy has ridges, or wales, of this pile that run the length of the fabric. Fine or pinwale corduroy has sixteen ridges to the inch, while wide wale corduroy has eight ridges to the inch. Broadwale corduroy, which has a velvety soft feel, may have only three wales to the inch, and no wale corduroy has an almost velvet-like feel. Prized for its comfort and practicality, corduroy fabric is used to make all sorts of clothing, from baby clothes to stylish suits, and is a popular upholstery fabric for furniture.

Corduroy first became popular in France and England in the 1700s, where it was named *corde du roi,* or "cord of the king." Though it was first woven of silk and was used to make clothing for royal servants, many think that the name *corde du roi* was actually made up by a British manufacturer who wished to glamorize his fabric with celebrity appeal. By the late 1800s corduroy was being woven of cotton and mass-produced in factories in both Europe and the United States. Durable yet inexpensive, cotton corduroy clothing became very popular with the working class. In 1918 auto manufacturer Henry Ford (1863–1947) chose hard-wearing, luxurious corduroy as upholstery in his new Ford Model T automobile.

Since the 1950s corduroy has been in and out of style several times and has been worn by all classes and types of people. Between periods of popularity corduroy has often been mocked as old-fashioned and out-of-date, but each decade has seen the fabric return, each time slightly updated. In the 1950s and 1960s corduroy was stereotyped as the fabric used in sport coats with leather patches at the elbows, worn by pipe-smoking college professors. During the late 1960s and 1970s, however, corduroy increased in popularity. In 1966 Jerry Garcia (1942–1995) of the rock group the Grateful Dead frequently wore corduroy pants and shirts on stage, which increased the demand for corduroy clothes among a whole generation of rebellious youth. The faded, worn look of the 1960s gave way to splashy color in the 1970s, and jeans manufacturers responded with "cords" or corduroy jeans in a wide variety of colors.

After the 1970s corduroy was not considered fashionable, even though in 1982 popular fashion designer Gianni Versace (1946–1997) introduced an entire line of men's clothing in corduroy. In the late 1990s a "new" corduroy was once again introduced, this time with spandex added for stretch, or no wales for a rich velvety look.

FOR MORE INFORMATION

Holch, Allegra. "Wale Watch." *WWD* (May 1, 1996): 6–8.

"It's Okay to Wear Corduroy. Really." *Esquire* (September 1999): 131–35.

Down Vests and Jackets

Down is a natural fiber found on waterfowl such as ducks and geese. These birds have a layer of fluffy feathers known as down underneath their regular feathers that traps air and helps the animal keep warm, even in icy water. Plucked off the bird and sewn between layers of fabric, down becomes an excellent insulation in human clothing, mattresses, and sleeping bags.

Many people have recognized and used the insulating quality of down. Even before the arrival of explorer Christopher Columbus (1451–1506) in the New World in 1492, Native Americans were known to use a mixture of wool and down to make warm blankets, and down and feathers were used for centuries to make warm, soft mattresses. The first manufactured down garment was made by Seattle, Washington, outdoorsman Eddie Bauer (1899–1986) in 1936. After he almost died on a winter fishing expedition, Bauer designed and marketed the Skyliner, a down-insulated jacket. The jacket was so effective in combating cold weather that Bauer made flight jackets and other down clothing for the military during World War II (1939–45).

An orange down vest. Since down is an insulation material, the fabric that covers it has been able to change with the style of the times. *Reproduced by permission of © Trinette Reed/CORBIS.*

It was not until the late 1960s, however, that down jackets and vests first caught the public imagination. Skiers such as 1968 American Olympic bronze medallist Suzy Chaffee (1946–) had glamour and flamboyance, and they wore brightly colored down vests and jackets. These soon became widely popular, especially the vests, which were a very practical design for those who were active out in cold weather. The wild colors and bright designs fit in well with the styles of the 1970s. At first mainly popular in areas like Colorado and the Pacific Northwest, which were known for outdoor sports, down was soon seen everywhere.

Because of its practicality as an insulation material, down remained very much in fashion after the 1970s, changing with the style of the times. In 1985, for example, classic raincoat manufacturer London Fog introduced a down jacket. Synthetic, or man-made, alternatives to down were also invented, such as 3M's Thinsulate and DuPont's Hollofil.

The 1990s saw a new rise in popularity for down, as inner-city youth began to buy "bubble jackets" or "fat jackets," nicknames for puffy down jackets. Noting the popularity of Eddie Bauer down jackets among urban young people, companies like Turbo Sportswear began to design hip down jackets with brand names like Triple F.A.T. Goose, South Pole, and First Down.

FOR MORE INFORMATION

Allstetter, Billy. "Triple F.A.T Goose Heads to the Suburbs After Becoming a Hit on Inner-City Streets." *Adweek's Marketing Week* (February 12, 1990): 17–19.

Tierney, John. "Phat City Can't Last, Fashion Archaeologists Say." *The New York Times* (January 21, 1999): B1.

Fringe

Native American tribes of the Plains and elsewhere had long created garments with fringe, which served as a type of gutter that repelled rainwater from the wearer. Fringe was a border or edge of hanging threads, cords, or strips, and was often found on garments made from suede, leather, and buckskin. Fringe first became a decorative fashion embellishment in the 1920s as part of the flapper look, a popular dress style for women. Skirts suddenly rose above the knee for the first time in Western history, and fringe was used to add a bit of length to the daring styles. But the use of Native American fringe was an outgrowth of the hippie movement of the late 1960s, a youth movement that stressed the rejection of mainstream values and a relaxation of standards of morality and personal conduct. The movement had a huge impact on mainstream society. Young Americans of the era were keenly interested in civil rights. The political gains made by African Americans earlier in the decade had spurred interest in the plight of other oppressed minority groups, including Native Americans. Wearing fringe became a way of showing sympathy for the Native American cause.

The 1969 Hollywood film *Easy Rider* helped popularize the fringe look as a fashion statement more than a political one. The tale of two drifters who "dropped out" of society, the cult hit featured unique clothing styles. The stars, Peter Fonda (c. 1939–) and Dennis Hopper (1936–), wore casual jackets, and Hopper's fringed brown suede jacket produced an artful effect when he rode his motorcycle. Fringed vests made from brown buckskin were also quite popular at the time, and a store called Tepee Town in Midtown Manhattan offered these and many other Indian looks, including moccasin boots and beaded belts. Designer Giorgio di Sant'Angelo (1933–1989) copied parts of elaborate Native American ceremonial dress for his fall 1970 collection. His designs won the prestigious Coty American Fashion Critics' Award. A backlash began around this time, championed by Native American folk singer Buffy Sainte-Marie (1941–). She deemed the wearing of such items insensitive to Native Americans of the contemporary era, many of whom lived in great poverty. By the mid-1970s fringe had mainly gone out of style.

FOR MORE INFORMATION

Ickeringill, Nan. "We're Stealing from the Indians, Again." *New York Times* (July 22, 1968): 38.

"The Indian Style." *Look* (October 20, 1970): 42–49.

Klemesrud, Judy. "Fighting a War on Behalf of Indians." *New York Times* (October 24, 1970): 20.

■ Gaucho Pants

Gaucho pants are wide-legged trousers for women with a cuff that ends around mid calf. Taking their name from pants once worn by South American cowboys, they were in style for a brief period in the early to mid-1970s. They were similar to the culotte short or skort, but gauchos were longer and meant to serve as a more formal, workplace-friendly alternative to skirts and slacks.

YVES SAINT LAURENT

French designer Yves Saint Laurent (1936–) was born in Oran, Algeria, and, at age seventeen, settled in Paris, France. There he attempted to secure work as a fashion and costume designer. Two years later, after the publication of several of his sketches, he was invited to meet the celebrated designer Christian Dior (1905–1957). Dior immediately hired the young designer and became his mentor. Then Dior suddenly died. At the age of twenty-one Saint Laurent was designated Dior's successor, becoming chief designer at the House of Dior.

Saint Laurent scored a major success with his first show, in which he presented what was dubbed the "trapeze" look. Trapeze skirts were flat-fronted and flared out from the waist in an almost triangular fashion. In 1960 he launched the elegant "Beat Look," spotlighting knit sleeves, turtlenecks, and black leather jackets bordered in fur. Two years later Saint Laurent left the House of Dior and opened his own fashion house. He soon became an expert at adapting his haute couture (high fashion) designs for average, middle-class, style-conscious women.

The 1960s found Saint Laurent offering additional innovative designs: the Mondrian dress (1965), which borrowed the geometrical shapes found in the paintings of Dutch artist Piet Mondrian (1872–1944); "le smoking," an androgynous, or gender-neutral, women's tuxedo/smoking jacket (1966); and the jumpsuit, a one-piece suit consisting of shirt and pants or shorts (1968). He designed pea coats, safari jackets, peasant blouses and dresses, and see-through blouses. He incorporated pop art into his designs, which during the 1960s was a trendy art style that included such familiar images as product packaging and newspaper comic strips. In 1966 he started a line of Rive Gauche ready-to-wear (off-the-rack versus custom-made) clothing, and he began designing menswear in 1974. Over the decades, the Yves Saint Laurent (or "YSL") name has been licensed to a range of products, including eyeglasses, bath and bed linens, furs, and perfume. He also was

French designer Yves Saint Laurent (1936–) was the first to popularize a more masculine look for women's wear. His trouser suits and *le smoking* tuxedo jacket quickly caught on with fashion-conscious women after 1968. Over the next few years sales of trousers skyrocketed over dresses and skirts. The boom was helped by the women's liberation movement, with its acceptance of unconventional roles for women. Bans against wearing pants to formal events and in the workplace declined considerably, making room for gaucho pants. The pants were borrowed from the costume of the pampas cowboy in Argentina and Uruguay. These cowboys, called gauchos, achieved mythic status for their riding skills and fierce independence in the eighteenth and nineteenth centuries. Though somewhat unusual in cut, gaucho pants reflected the growing interest in ethnic looks and world cultures in the late 1960s and 1970s. Fashion writers praised them as one of the new, modern alternatives to skirts.

the first major designer to employ models of varied ethnic backgrounds.

From the late 1960s on, more and more women entered the workplace. To accommodate their needs, Saint Laurent designed work attire that included pants and blazers rather than skirts and dresses. These innovations were not immediately accepted. At first, the classic Saint Laurent pantsuit was not considered appropriate workplace apparel for women. Occasionally, women wearing them were turned away from fancier restaurants.

In 1983 the Museum of Modern Art in New York City presented an exhibit spotlighting a quarter-century of Saint Laurent's creations. It was the first time a still-active designer was so honored. In October 1998 Saint Laurent introduced his final ready-to-wear collection, and the following year he sold his business to Gucci. Saint Laurent announced his retirement in 2002. Yves Saint Laurent's life and career may be summed up by what is perhaps his most celebrated declaration: "Fashions fade, style is eternal."

Yves Saint Laurent, left, designed clothes that made women look and feel fashionable and stunning. *Reproduced by permission of © Reuters NewMedia Inc./CORBIS.*

Gauchos first made an impact in the fall of 1970. American designer Anne Klein (1923–1974) offered gray flannel gauchos that appeared in an August 30, 1970, issue of the *New York Times Magazine*'s twice-yearly fashion supplement. They soon caught on with the mass-market apparel sellers. Often they were shown with boots, another new trend in women's wear of the era. Within a few years, however, gauchos had declined in popularity. The mid-calf length broke the line of the leg, and they seemed to give the wearer a wider silhouette, or shape, than desired. Unflattering to most, they eventually became synonymous with some of the decade's more ill-advised fashion fads.

FOR MORE INFORMATION

"Fashions of the Times." *New York Times Magazine* (August 30, 1970): 62.

Herald, Jacqueline. *Fashions of a Decade: The 1970s.* New York: Facts on File, 1992.

Morris, Bernadine. "You Don't Like Midiskirts? There Are Always Gaucho Pants." *New York Times* (April 29, 1970): 36.

Rawsthorn, Alice. *Yves Saint Laurent: A Biography.* New York: HarperCollins, 1996.

Saint Laurent, Yves. *Yves Saint Laurent: Images of Design 1958–1988.* New York: Knopf, 1988.

Saint Laurent, Yves, Diana Vreeland, et al. *Yves Saint Laurent.* New York: Museum of Modern Art, 1983.

Halter Tops

The halter top, on the model at right, was based on the neckline of some Asian clothing.
Reproduced by permission of © Genevieve Naylor/CORBIS.

A sleeveless triangular top that ties around the back and at the back of the neck, the halter top loosely covers the breasts and chest, while leaving bare the shoulders, upper back, and sometimes the midriff, the area below the breasts and above the waist. The halter top was at the peak of its popularity during the late 1960s and 1970s.

First seen as a dramatic neckline on formal gowns in the 1930s, the halter top was based on the sleeveless, high-necked design of some Asian clothing. The halter top appeared again during the 1940s, this time on the beach as part of a two-piece bathing suit popularized by movie stars such as Betty Grable (1916–1973). The simplicity of design made the halter top easy to make at home, and the small amount of fabric required made it a good choice during World War II (1939–45), when the demands of war limited the supply of cloth.

By the late 1960s the rise of youth culture and movements for women's rights and civil rights impacted fashion. A new informality and naturalness was in style, and women began to shed the tight, cumbersome undergarments that they had long been expected to wear. The rise of feminism, an organized movement advocating for female equality, also contributed to women's desire for freedom from constricting clothing. The first garment to go was the girdle, and the brassiere soon followed. The new braless look was perfect for a revival of the halter top.

Halter tops were casual, comfortable, and playfully sexy and soon became a staple of many young women's wardrobe. Like the women of the 1940s, women of the 1960s appreciated how easy it was to make one's own halter tops. Some even tied scarves or bandannas together for an inexpensive and simple, but exotic, look. Manufacturers, of course, picked up the trend and stores began selling halter tops in a wide variety of colors, fabrics, and styles. Some halter tops came almost to the waist, covering most of the midriff, while others stopped just under the breasts for maximum skin exposure. The halter top design was also used to make an elegant top for dresses and jumpsuits, which were one-piece outfits that combined pants and top. Sexy female celebrities like Cher (1946–) and actress Goldie Hawn (1945–) were pictured in halter tops, which made even more women want to buy them.

Halter tops did go out of fashion after the 1970s, though many women continued to wear them for beachwear and other informal summer occasions. They were revived as high fashion in the mid-1990s, when popular singers like Britney Spears (1981–) and Mariah Carey (1969–) tied on the revealing halters.

FOR MORE INFORMATION

Powe-Temperley, Kitty. *20th Century Fashion: The 1960s, Mods and Hippies.* Milwaukee, WI: Gareth Stevens, 2000.

Hip Huggers

Hip huggers are tightly fitted pants whose waistline has been dropped below the natural waist of the wearer. Hip huggers usually have flared or bell-bottom legs, and the dropped waist can vary from hanging modestly just below the waist to a sitting several inches below the navel. Hip huggers often have no built-in waistband but are frequently worn with wide belts. First worn by the "mods," British fashion trendsetters of the 1960s, hip huggers were popular with both men and women throughout the 1970s. They have come back into fashion several times since, both as 1970s nostalgia and as new designer fashions in the early twenty-first century.

During the late 1960s and early 1970s, hip huggers were widely worn by young people, from high school students to hippies, youth who rebelled against the norms of society. The so-called sexual revolution of the times called for a freer, looser style with regard to expressing one's sexuality, and sexy, revealing hip huggers fit in perfectly. While the first hip huggers exposed only the navel, more extreme designs were produced, which barely covered the wearer's bottom. Low-slung hip hugger pants exposed the bare midriff (the area below the breasts and above the waist) on both men and women. Rock stars, such as the Rolling Stones and 1970s husband and wife team Sonny (1935–1998) and Cher (1946–), popularized hip huggers by wearing them on stage.

While mods wore hip huggers in bold, geometric prints, and hippies wore them in ragged denim, the disco dancers of the late 1970s brought glitz to the hip hugger. Tight, low hip huggers in shiny fabrics, such as satin, and bright colors were seen on popular singers of the time, from Donna Summer (1948–) to Rod Stewart (1945–).

Hip huggers retained some degree of popularity after the 1970s but almost exclusively among young women. In the 1990s British fashion designer Alexander McQueen (c. 1969–) introduced ultra-low-cut hip huggers that were quickly dubbed "bum pants" because they exposed so much of the wearers' bums, the British slang for buttocks. The very low and tight hip huggers popularized by pop music singers such as Britney Spears (1981–) and Christina Aguilera (1980–) remained popular into the

Hip huggers made their debut in the 1960s and were again popular in the early twenty-first century. They often sat well below the navel. *Reproduced by permission of © Mauro Panci/ CORBIS.*

early twenty-first century. The year 2000 also saw the introduction of a kind of "false" hip hugger with a high waist and a wide belt set low on the hips, giving the illusion of the low cut, while covering more of the body.

Because hip huggers are so revealing they have sometimes been banned. Even the medical profession has had its reservations about them, with some doctors asserting that tight hip hugger pants cause a condition called paresthesia, or nerve damage in the wearer's thighs.

FOR MORE INFORMATION

Herald, Jacqueline. *Fashions of a Decade: The 1970s.* Edited by Elane Feldman and Valerie Cumming. New York: Facts on File, 1992.

Hot Pants

Hot pants are extremely short shorts that were designed to be worn as dressy clothing for women. Young people of the 1970s began to leave behind the ragged, patched-denim political style of the mid- to late 1960s. They gathered in nightclubs to dance to disco music and returned to the glamorous styles made popular in Great Britain in the early 1960s by youths known as "mods." Many fashion experts see hot pants as a natural development of the rising miniskirt. Skirts became so short that they exposed the underwear, so a sort of formal short pair of shorts, known as short shorts, came into style. The new shorts were considered shocking and slightly naughty, and *Women's Wear Daily,* an influential fashion magazine, gave them the name hot pants. Unlike ordinary shorts, hot pants were usually made from formal fabrics such as velvet, satin, or leather.

Short, sexy pants had been seen before, as far back as the 1920s and 1930s, especially in Europe, but they had mainly been worn by prostitutes and nightclub performers. In the 1930 German film *The Blue Angel,* Marlene Dietrich (c. 1901–1992) played Lola Lola, a seductive nightclub singer who shows off her legs in a pair of extremely short shorts that are an obvious ancestor of hot pants. Comic book heroine Wonder Woman was also costumed in short shorts with high boots, a fashion that accurately predicted the 1970s look of hot pants paired with boots or platform shoes.

Though not everyone had the courage to wear the revealing new fashion, hot pants were popular among thin young women who wished to keep up-to-date in the extravagantly flashy climate of the 1970s. For a short time they even became part of the official flight attendants' uniform for Allegheny Airlines (a subsidiary of US Airways). Rhythm-and-blues singer James Brown (c. 1928–) released a popular song titled "Hot Pants" in 1977.

Hot pants went out of fashion within a few years of their introduction, and they are usually remembered as one of the many fashion mistakes of the 1970s. Since the end of that decade the look has been seldom seen, though sometimes they have been spotted on fashion models and celebrities. However, hot pants did feature prominently in the early 1980s television show *The Dukes of Hazzard* (1979–85), in which the female lead wore short denim shorts that came to be known as "Daisy Dukes" after her character.

FOR MORE INFORMATION

Steele, Valerie. *Fifty Years of Fashion: New Look to Now.* New Haven, CT: Yale University Press, 1997.

Jogging Suits

When the sport of jogging became a national obsession in the 1970s, bringing with it a fascination with fitness, people were looking for appropriate attire for running along city streets and country lanes, or jogging in place at the gym. Baseball, football, basketball, and hockey players had uniforms that were designed for the specifics of their sport and runners were looking for the same. Casual street clothes such as jeans and a loosely-fitted shirt were impractical. The old T-shirt and shorts or one-piece cotton gym suit was not fashionable. Out of this need came the popularity of the jogging suit: a casual two-piece outfit designed and marketed for men and women that included a zip jacket and elastic-waist pants.

The first jogging suits consisted of clothing that already existed: fleece sweatpants and hooded sweatshirts. As an athletic ensemble, it was an offshoot of the traditional tracksuit, which had been in existence since the early 1950s. The tracksuit was made up of long pants and a long-sleeved jacket and was worn by runners and other athletes. For the style-conscious, however, such attire seemed drab. Realizing that a market was emerging for a stylish jogging wardrobe,

Jogging suits—even among nonathletes—have been an American fashion staple since the 1970s. *Reproduced by permission of © Tom Stewart/CORBIS.*

designers created what came to be known as the jogging suit. Jogging suits were created for comfort and fabric breathability, which meant that air flowed easily through the fabric, keeping the wearer from getting too hot. They were made of velour, nylon, polar fleece, and polyester and were stitched together so as to withstand wear and the elements.

In 1975 Adidas introduced its top-selling nylon and polyester jogging suit. It consisted of a full-zip jacket with two front pockets and a ribbed neck, hem, and cuffs. The pants featured an internal drawcord, ankle zippers, and elastic side-seam pockets. A three-stripe design was added to the jacket sleeves and pant side seams. The suit had the embroidered company logo on the left hip of the pants and the left breast of the jacket. The women's model was practically identical, except for the tailoring.

Not everyone purchased jogging suits for running. Some wore them as sportswear, because they were sleek and attractive. Jogging suits thus became a fashion trend, with designers such as Russian-born Oleg Cassini (1913–) joining the athletic wear companies in marketing them. In the 1980s and 1990s the jogging suit evolved into the contemporary tracksuit: smoother, more fitted, and shinier, and made of state-of-the-art nylon and spandex materials. While many people actually exercised in these outfits, tracksuits were popularized by rap artists and other musicians and dancers as a type of urban street fashion.

FOR MORE INFORMATION

Schnurnberger, Lynn. *Let There Be Clothes: 40,000 Years of Fashion.* New York: Workman Publishing, 1991.

Leisure Suits

Leisure suits, which gained popularity among men during the 1970s, were casual suits consisting of matching jacket and trousers. They were made of polyester fabric, often in bright colors or earth tone plaids. The leisure suit jacket was distinctively

DISCO

During the 1970s rock music dance clubs became extremely popular. Young people, wearing polyester bell-bottoms and platform shoes, lined up outside popular clubs for a chance to enter dance floors lit with bright, pulsing lights and dance to recorded music with a pounding beat. Disco was the word that described the clubs, the music, the dance style, and the fashions that grew out of the scene.

A discotheque is a dance club that plays music on records, or discs, rather than having a live band. Discotheques got their start in Paris, France, during World War II (1939–45), when France was occupied by the German army. In an effort to control rebellious young people, the Germans made popular jazz music illegal, so many French youth gathered in secret clubs to dance to recordings of the music they loved. One of these clubs was called La Discotheque. In the 1960s Paris was also the home of another internationally famous discotheque, the Whiskey a Go-Go, which loaned its name to go-go boots, short, white boots popular among mod women, and go-go dancers, who performed in nightclubs.

Disco dancing gained tremendous popularity during the 1970s. Young people of the times often felt overwhelmed by the social problems around them, and they sought a more carefree lifestyle. Dancing became a favorite leisure activity. Unlike the dance clubs of previous times, disco dance clubs attracted people of mixed racial and sexual orientations. People of color and whites, gays and heterosexuals alike danced to driving rhythms, often created by drum machines. Disc jockeys, or deejays, mixed the records on two or three turntables to make each song last as long as possible. As the popularity of the dancing clubs grew, major record companies began to seek out and record disco artists, even releasing long-playing records to duplicate the deejays' long versions of songs.

John Travolta in a scene from the trendsetting 1977 disco film *Saturday Night Fever*. *Reproduced by permission of The Kobal Collection.*

In 1977 the film *Saturday Night Fever* was released, starring John Travolta (1954–) as a young working-class man who seeks love and success on the disco dance floor. The popularity of the movie *Saturday Night Fever* and its soundtrack with songs by the Bee Gees helped spread the disco craze around the world.

When disco grew to mass popularity by the late 1970s, those who wanted to be hip turned to new forms of music. An anti-disco craze began at the same time, with rock radio stations leading a "Disco sucks!" campaign. By the early 1980s most experts declared that disco was dead. Though many people lump disco in with bell-bottoms and leisure suits as another tasteless 1970s fad, disco has survived into the twenty-first century in different forms of driving dance music such as electronica, techno, house, and Latin freestyle.

styled, with an open front with large collar and lapels, large patch pockets, and stitching in a color that contrasted with the fabric. Beginning in the early 1960s, fashion designers experimented with stylish and casual suits for men in an effort to modernize men's fashions to keep pace with women's changing styles. French designers Pierre Cardin (1922–) and Yves Saint Laurent (1936–) both introduced modern looks for men. Cardin's collarless suit, made famous by the British pop band the Beatles, and Saint Laurent's "safari suit," were both forerunners of the leisure suit, which offered men casual, stylish looks that soon developed into the distinctive styling of the leisure suit.

In 1970 American designer Jerry Rosengarten (c. 1945–) invented a new style of suit that paired a shirt jacket with matching pants to demonstrate the usefulness of a new double-knit polyester fabric. Pants maker Lee Jeans marketed Rosengarten's design in a line for men and boys called LEEsures. Influenced by the extremely informal style associated with the hippies, a group of young people who rejected conventional values and dress, men of the 1970s wanted to be able to dress more casually. Leisure suits were marketed to these buyers as comfortable business suits. Though they were never really accepted as business dress, they did become popular for parties, discos, and other social events. Mothers especially liked the new suits for their young sons, because the polyester fabric was extremely durable and easy to care for.

Often worn with brightly patterned polyester shirts, gold chains and medallions, and vinyl platform shoes, leisure suits were briefly very popular. Perhaps the most famous leisure suit was worn by actor John Travolta (1954–) when he starred as a disco dancer in the film *Saturday Night Fever* (1977). Before too long, however, there was a backlash against the suits. Some upscale restaurants began to post signs forbidding the suits, and they gradually fell out of fashion. Leisure suits have endured, however, as a symbol of 1970s fashion extremes. In the twenty-first century fans of retro fashion gathered for leisure suit conventions to show off the bright polyester costumes that they would hardly dare to wear anywhere else.

FOR MORE INFORMATION

Adato, Allison, and David Burnett. "A Leisure Suit Convention." *Life* (February 1996): 18–21.

Stern, Jane, and Michael Stern. *The Encyclopedia of Bad Taste.* New York: HarperCollins, 1990.

[*See also* **Volume 4, 1930–45: Men's Suits**]

The miniskirt was stylish, provocative, fun, and sexy. *Reproduced by permission of © Bettmann/CORBIS.*

Miniskirt

The miniskirt was introduced in 1965 at the fashion show of French designer André Courreges (1923–). He felt that the design of women's clothes was not keeping up with the modern trends of the 1950s and 1960s and wanted to introduce a look that was modern, streamlined, and easy. His miniskirts were A-line skirts, narrow at the waist and wider at the hem, that ended four inches above the knee.

The audience at Courreges's show greeted his new designs in shocked silence, but it would not be long before fashion critics and women themselves embraced the exciting modern look. Meanwhile, in London, fashion designer Mary Quant (1934–) also began to sell a new look for the modern woman. In 1955 Quant had opened a London boutique called Bazaar in which she sold designer clothes that could be worn by the average person, not just fashion models. Shortly after Courreges had revealed his line of clothes, Quant introduced her own miniskirt, a tightly fitted skirt with an even shorter hemline, up to the middle of the thigh.

JACQUELINE KENNEDY

Few public figures have had more effect on American style, fashion, and culture in general than Jacqueline Kennedy (1929–1994) did during the early 1960s, when she was married to John Fitzgerald Kennedy (1917–1963), the thirty-fifth president of the United States. Though she disliked the spotlight of public life, Jacqueline took her responsibilities as first lady seriously and created an atmosphere of elegance and dignity that surrounded her husband's presidency. A quiet, reserved woman from an upper-class family whose poise and grace charmed people of all classes both in the United States and abroad, Jacqueline had a confident, modern style that inspired women all over the world to imitate her.

Born Jacqueline Bouvier in 1929 in South Hampton, New York, she was raised in a socially prominent family. She attended Miss Porter's, an exclusive girl's school in Connecticut, where she loved riding horses. The horsewoman's style of tailored slacks and jackets would become one of

Jacqueline's fashion trademarks. In 1953 Jacqueline Bouvier married Massachusetts congressman John Kennedy and entered the political life. By 1960 the couple and their two children had moved into the White House. The handsome John Kennedy was the youngest man to be elected president, and he and Jacqueline brought a welcome feeling of youth and energy to a country entering a new decade. Because of the new medium of television, citizens could watch the president and his wife more closely than ever before, and the new first couple was extremely popular. Raised in the upper class and educated in Europe, Jacqueline knew about the latest Paris fashions. She loved simple, elegant designs, and brought that elegance and sophistication to the White House.

As the wife of the president, Jacqueline was the most watched woman in the country, and her clothing instantly became famous. She became known for her bouffant hairstyle and the small, round hats, called pillbox hats, that designer Halston (1932–1990) created for her. She left behind the puffy skirts of the 1950s, and Oleg

Quant's miniskirt became part of a new "mod" style, named after the reigning fashion among British youth in the 1960s. Courreges and Quant both paired miniskirts with flat white boots and geometric prints, and celebrities like British model Twiggy (1946–) and French actress and sex symbol Brigitte Bardot (1934–) popularized the new look. Soon the new short skirts were seen on such respectable figures as American first lady Jacqueline Kennedy (1929–1994).

Over the years minis kept getting shorter, becoming the micromini and even the micro-micro. The average woman did not wear the most extreme styles, but the miniskirt did begin a trend of shorter skirts and a freer, more relaxed style for women. Rather than being expected to keep themselves covered up, modern women of the 1960s were presented in a style that was bold, sexy, and fun.

Cassini (1913–) designed her simple A-line suits in striking colors, which were widely imitated. Always an active sportswoman, Jacqueline was confident enough to dress casual, and she became known for wearing slacks, shorts, and riding clothes, at a time when most women wore skirts and dresses in public. Many American women imitated the first lady's look of tapered slacks and casual fitted tops, worn with a scarf tied around the hair and big sunglasses.

Jacqueline Kennedy's international, sophisticated style was not only imitated in the United States but around the world. Even after the tragic assassination of President Kennedy in 1963, Jacqueline Kennedy never really left public life, though she tried. People worldwide were still fascinated by her, and tabloid newspapers and aggressive celebrity photographers called paparazzi followed her everywhere, hoping for a picture or a story. In 1968 she married Greek millionaire Aristotle Onassis (c. 1900–1975), and after his death in 1975 she worked as a book editor and lived with a companion, Maurice Templeton. She died of cancer in 1994.

Jacqueline Kennedy Onassis.

Hemlines have gone up and down several times since 1965, and the miniskirt has been reintroduced several times, notably in the 1980s when singer Madonna's (1958–) short skirts popularized the mini again among young women.

FOR MORE INFORMATION

Crawford, Nigel. *Key Moments in Fashion.* New York: Sterling Publishing, 2001.

Powe-Temperley, Kitty. *20th Century Fashion: The 1960s, Mods and Hippies.* Milwaukee, WI: Gareth Stevens, 2000.

Quant, Mary. *Quant by Quant.* New York: Putnam, 1966.

Schneider, Karen. "Up, Up, and Hooray! Designer Andre Courreges Celebrates 25 Years of Miniskirt Fame." *People Weekly* (July 9, 1990): 79–82.

Nehru Jacket

Young people of the 1960s who were unhappy with the culture and values they had grown up with began to explore other cultures, seeking different points of view. Because many of these young people opposed war and sought peaceful solutions, they admired the people of India, who had achieved independence from the British Empire in 1947 through largely nonviolent means.

In 1964 the first prime minister of independent India, pacifist Jawaharlal Nehru (1889–1964), was pictured in *Vogue* magazine wearing his traditional coat. *Vogue* was an important fashion influence, and the Nehru jacket, named after Prime Minister Nehru, started to gain popularity. The distinctive Nehru jacket is a close-fitted, single-breasted (one row of buttons down the front) coat with a stand-up collar and no lapels. Around the same time, the popular British rock group the Beatles traveled to India to study meditation techniques, and soon the group's members began wearing Nehru jackets and setting a new fashion trend.

The jackets became popular very quickly. Celebrities from talk show host Johnny Carson (1925–) to football star Joe Namath (1943–) wore Nehru jackets, and singer Sammy Davis Jr. (1925–1990) was reported to own two hundred of them. Nehru jackets were made from a wide variety of materials besides plain cotton and wool, including brocade, vinyl, and sharkskin.

The Nehru jacket fad ended within just a few years. Suddenly the Nehru jacket became a symbol not only of dated and out-of-style clothing, but also of the type of person who still wore the jacket. The Nehru jacket came to represent an aging loser, trying unsuccessfully to be hip and cool, an image that has persisted for decades. In 1994 the rock group Love Battery released the song "Nehru Jacket," in which a man in bell-bottoms and a Nehru jacket unsuccessfully tries to get a date. In the Austin Powers movies of the late 1990s and early 2000s, about a spy who is frozen in the 1960s and thawed out in the 1990s, Austin Powers's Nehru jacket is used to express his geeky hipness and awkwardness.

In fashion, however, what is considered outdated by one generation becomes trendy for another. In the late 1990s the Nehru jacket began to appear in fashion magazines again as a desirable garment for both women and men. In 2002 fashion designer Ermenegildo Zegna designed a "guru suit" with a Nehru jacket, and former U.S. president Bill Clinton (1946–) was seen in a tuxedo with a Nehru jacket in the summer of 2001.

FOR MORE INFORMATION

O'Hara, Georgina. *The Encyclopedia of Fashion from 1840 to the 1980s.* London, England: Thames and Hudson, 1986.

Painter's Pants

Blue collar or utilitarian chic is the name given to the fashion trend of work clothes becoming high fashion. Like blue jeans, painter's pants were discovered as a fashion item by those who never wore them for work. Originally designed to be worn by working painters, painter's pants have been sold by makers of work clothes such as Dickies, since at least the 1920s. Made of white canvas with heavily stitched seams, painter's pants are distinguished by their many pockets, some roomy enough to hold brushes and rags, others small enough to keep a putty knife or screwdriver close at hand. Painter's pants also have a hammer loop, a fabric strap sized to hold the handle of a hammer, on the right-hand leg seam. Many young women, energized by the Women's and Gay Liberation movements of the early 1970s, wore painter's pants as a political statement, often with work boots, because they were the clothes of skilled tradespeople and had been formerly reserved for men.

However, painter's pants became especially fashionable during the late 1970s. The white pants were themselves a blank canvas, and soon both men and women were painting, spattering, and embroidering their painter's pants to make individual fashion statements. Bright, paint-splashed painter's pants were in perfect harmony with the florescent colors and vivid patterns that were popular at the time. Some people even made playful use of the hammer loop by hanging a toy hammer or bright bandanna there. Painter's hats and overalls were also decorated for street wear. Soon clothing manufacturers caught onto the demand for stylish painter's pants and began to manufacture them in pastels and bright colors, as well as the popular splattered paint design.

During the 1980s when many 1970s fashions were ridiculed, painter's pants had a slight decrease in popularity, but by the 1990s they had returned to favor again as high fashion. Several fashion designers, such as Victor Alfaro (1963–), featured clean, white painter's pants in their collections.

FOR MORE INFORMATION

Romero, Elena. "Workwear Is Music to YM Market." *Daily News Record* (July 2, 1996): 8–9.

Vargo, Julie. "Dickies: Dressing Men at Work for 75 Years." *Daily News Record* (November 3, 1997):12–14.

Pantsuit

Before the late 1960s women only wore pants while working in the garden or around the house, engaging in such female-approved sports as bowling, or traveling to the beach. In most any business, school, or formal public or social setting women were expected to wear skirts or dresses. As feminism, the social movement to gain full and equal rights for women, grew more powerful in the 1960s and women increased their presence in the workplace, the notion that females and skirts were synonymous was viewed as impractical and outdated. French designer Yves Saint Laurent (1936–) and other top designers responded to this desire for skirt-liberation by creating the pantsuit: an outfit, designed and tailored specifically for women, comprised of matching slacks and jacket. By the mid-1960s nearly all the important Paris, France, designers were creating and marketing pantsuits. Pantsuits allowed women in the workplace the opportunity to enjoy the mobility and flexibility they lacked when wearing a dress or skirt.

Some pantsuits were female versions of traditional male suits. They featured solid colors, blacks and blues and browns, or came in plaid or tweed. Others were more traditionally feminine, designed in pastel colors or even in white lace over pink. Jackets came in varying lengths and were single or double-breasted. Pants were narrow, tapered, or flared. The suits were made of a range of materials, such as wool, suede, leather, twill, velvet, silk, cotton, polyester, and cotton-polyester blends. Unlike their male counterparts, women accessorized their pantsuits with necklaces, pins, gloves, scarves, and designer handbags and shoes.

Pantsuits were not immediately accepted as formal social or workplace attire. Younger women began wearing them and were scornfully viewed not only by the male establishment but by their older female coworkers as well. Exclusive restaurants refused to seat women dressed in even the most stylish and expensive pantsuits. Eventually, workplace and restaurant dress codes were altered to accommodate women wearing them.

FOR MORE INFORMATION

Molloy, John T. *New Women's Dress for Success.* New York: Warner Books, 1996.

Women wearing pantsuits, like the one here, were sometimes banned from restaurants that resisted the feminist movement and saw pants as too masculine. *Reproduced by permission of AP/Wide World Photos.*

Pantyhose

People have worn some sort of stockings or socks for centuries, the style varying somewhat as fashions and technology changed and developed. In the 1800s women usually wore cotton stockings, which were covered by their long skirts, but by the 1920s hemlines had risen, and sheer silk stockings became popular. These were two individual tubes of silk, one for each leg. They were held up by garters, elastic circles that fitted tight around each leg, or garter belts, elastic bands that went around the waist with several fasteners that hung down to secure the stockings. Later, tight elastic pants called girdles would be outfitted with fasteners for stockings and worn for the dual purpose of keeping up hose and making a woman look slimmer.

In 1959 Allen Gant Sr., a designer for North Carolina clothing manufacturer Glen Raven Mills, created a garment that combined underpants and stockings. Although worn at first by dancers and other theater performers who wore skimpy costumes, pantyhose would become popular for all women by 1965. Several factors led to the increased popularity of pantyhose. First, Glen Raven Mills incorporated a new stretchy fabric called spandex into pantyhose, which helped the hose to keep their shape instead of becoming stretched out and baggy. Second, a London, England, fashion designer named Mary Quant (1934–) introduced a new, very short skirt, called the miniskirt. The tops of old-fashioned stockings held by garters showed under the new skirts, so women turned to pantyhose and most discarded their uncomfortable garter belts for good. Pantyhose became a multimillion-dollar industry.

Though pantyhose were once hailed as a giant innovation in women's fashion and a wonderful benefit for busy women, women continued to demand more comfort and freedom of dress. Even though skirts and pantyhose were still considered necessary for women in many places, pants had become increasingly accepted business and dress attire for women by the late 1970s. In the 1990s a general trend toward wearing more casual styles to work enticed many women to stop wearing pantyhose. The profits of the hosiery industry continued to fall into the early twenty-first century.

FOR MORE INFORMATION

Melinkoff, Ellen. *What We Wore.* New York: Quill Press, 1984.

"Nights of the Garter Are Over, 1959." *Wall Street Journal* (August 25, 1989): B1.

Peasant Look

During the late 1960s and early 1970s many young women rejected traditional fashion for more eccentric, original styles. One such style was the peasant look: a type of clothing that was an offshoot of the garments worn for centuries by the European lower classes. Peasant skirts and dresses were long and flowing. Skirts and blouses featured loose, off-the-shoulder necklines, split necklines styled to resemble tunics, or drawstrings that could be tied. The blouses were tucked in or not, depending upon personal preference. Peasant-style clothing often was loosely woven, using such natural fabrics as linen or soft, combed cotton. They featured solid colors; earth tones such as brown, tan, white, and ivory were especially popular. Blouses often were adorned with hand-done embroidery, and outfits were designed using floral patterns. The sleeves were soft and ruffled or bell-shaped. To a lesser extent young men also adopted the peasant look. Male peasant clothing included a collarless shirt, pants, and belt. The shirt was usually not tucked in.

For real peasants, of course, this style was no fashion statement. It existed for practical reasons: peasant-style clothing was easy to make and loosely fitted, allowing the wearer to work in the fields or on farms with maximum comfort. For modern young people, however, the style offered a romantic, bohemian (referring to a person who lives an unconventional lifestyle) feeling that made them feel they were different from the rest of society.

In 1976 famed designer Yves Saint Laurent (1936–) initiated what came to be known as the "Rich Peasant" or "Peasant Chic" look. These designs were characterized by drawstring blouses and long, full skirts with a gathered waistband called dirndl skirts, and they were conceived in earth tones. A Rich Peasant outfit featured fur trim and expensive knee-length boots made of calfskin, elements missing from earlier peasant attire. Add-ons included scarves, shawls, and vests. Saint Laurent's designs remained popular through the mid-1980s.

The peasant look, with its long, flowing garments decorated with embroidery or floral patterns, was extremely popular throughout the 1960s and 1970s and made a comeback in the late 1990s. *Reproduced by permission of AP/Wide World Photos/Fashion Wire Daily.*

The original, more basic peasant look enjoyed a revival in the late 1990s and early twenty-first century. In addition to the conventional fabrics, rayon and crushed velvet polyester were also popular.

FOR MORE INFORMATION

Holderness, Esther R. *Peasant Chic: A Guide to Making Unique Clothing Using Traditional Folk Designs.* New York: Hawthorn Books, 1977.

Tie-Dye

Worn by legions of hippies, tie-dye is perhaps the most enduring symbol of the 1960s. *Reproduced by permission of © Royalty-Free/ CORBIS.*

Tie-dyeing was especially popular with American youth who opposed the Vietnam War (1954–75), a controversial war in which the United States aided South Vietnam in its fight against a takeover by Communist North Vietnam. During the late 1960s American young people rebelled against the conservative rules of dress and appearance that had influenced their parents' generation, and many began to appreciate a movement that valued arts and crafts, simplicity, and traditional ways of making things. Tie-dye was a natural outgrowth of these values, combining personal creativity and bright designs to create low-cost clothing. Tie-dye was not a new invention; it has roots in Indian *bandhani* and Japanese *shibori,* both dyeing techniques that involve binding areas of fabric before dyeing to create color patterns. Indonesia, Nigeria, and Peru also have long traditions of tie-dyeing fabrics, as do many other countries.

To make a fashionable tie-dyed T-shirt, young people would wrap strings around crumpled shirts and dunk them in vats of inexpensive dye. Once dry the dyed T-shirts would display swirling patterns of color that rebellious American youth could be seen wearing with faded jeans and sandals. Popular rock musicians of the time, such as Jimi Hendrix (1942–1970) and John Sebastian (1944–), wore tie-dye on stage, increasing its popularity. The singer Janis Joplin (1943–1970) was said to sleep on tie-dyed satin sheets. Tie-dye was so popular during the 1960s that it has remained a symbol of trends and movements of the time: hippies (people who rejected the moral customs of established society), rock concerts, psychedelic drugs, and antiwar marches. At the same time, those who disliked the style and values of the hippies ridiculed tie-dye as a symbol of drug use, irresponsibility, and mindless rebellion.

During the 1980s, when many of the fashions of the 1960s and 1970s were rejected, tie-dye lost some of its popularity. One group, however, clung to tie-dye as their symbol throughout the 1980s and 1990s: the Deadheads. Deadheads were loyal fans of the rock group the Grateful Dead. Grateful Dead concerts became festivals of tie-dye, and those who brought and sold tie-dye clothing at the events became known as "dyes." After the Grateful Dead disbanded in 1995, concerts of other rock groups, such as Phish, became venues for wearing, selling, and exchanging tie-dye clothing.

Tie-dye became a mainstream fashion starting in the 1990s. Unlike the tie-dye of the 1960s, this modern tie-dye was often mass-produced and sold in retail shops at large malls. Some original tie-dye designs made on silk or rayon, however, were considered fashionable artwork and sold at high prices in designer boutiques. Despite its popularity in the 1990s and 2000s, the bright, swirling, one-of-kind nature of tie-dye continues to be identified with the nonconformist lifestyle of the hippies of the 1960s.

FOR MORE INFORMATION

Anderson, Brian, and Jennifer L. Zebel. "Grateful Clients Prefer Tie-Dye Apparel." *Wearables Business* (May 2000): 38–43.

Kreider, Katherine. *Tie-Dye.* Lincolnwood, IL: McGraw-Hill, 1989.

Powe-Temperley, Kitty. *20th Century Fashion: The 1960s, Mods and Hippies.* Milwaukee, WI: Gareth Stevens, 2000.

Velour

Velours is the French word for velvet, and, like velvet, velour is woven by a special process with looped threads that are cut to form a pile, or textured surface. What distinguishes velour from velvet is the fabric from which it is woven. While velvet is most often made of silk or the synthetic fabrics nylon or acetate, velour is loosely woven of cotton, sometimes blended with synthetic fiber.

Long used as a drapery and upholstery fabric, particularly in automobiles, velour, when it gained popularity as a fabric for clothing in the 1970s, was often ridiculed for its upholstery background. Once members of popular 1970s rock groups such as the Bee Gees wore it, however, many young people began to consider the fabric hip and modern. The popularity of velour in the 1970s also relied on the previous decade. During the 1960s young men had begun to rebel against the conservative dress of previous generations and started to wear more brightly colored, casual clothes. Such clothes became highly fashionable for the average man, and velour was sewn into comfortable shirts and pants for men and women alike.

The most recognized velour garment of the 1970s is the jogging suit worn by both men and women. Sportswear companies such as Adidas began to make brightly patterned velour into jogging suits, with a loosely fitted top and pants made of matching fabric. A modified version of the velour jogging suit was used to represent futuristic clothing on the science fiction television series *Star Trek* (1966–69), which reached its peak of popularity in syndication in the 1970s.

Like many distinctive 1970s fashions, velour went out of fashion during the 1980s as men returned to a more conservative, buttoned-down look. However, the fabric came back into fashion for both men and women in the twenty-first century and its popularity was given a boost when singer and actress Jennifer Lopez (1970–) introduced her own line of velour fashions.

FOR MORE INFORMATION

Gilmour, Sarah. *20th Century Fashion: The 70s, Punks, Glam Rockers, and New Romantics.* Milwaukee, WI: Gareth Stevens, 1999.

Wrap Dress

Diane von Furstenberg's (1946–) wrap dress was one of American fashion's top sellers during the first half of the 1970s. The one-piece, knee-length garment, which wrapped in the front and featured built-in string ties of the same fabric, tied around the waist and sold in stores for around eighty dollars. Made from colorful abstract prints that von Furstenberg designed herself, the dress caught on with legions of American women, and some five million were sold at their height of popularity. The success of this dress made von Furstenberg one of the first designers to succeed by appealing primarily to the mass market, instead of to the world of haute couture, or high fashion.

Von Furstenberg was in her mid-twenties in 1972 when she launched her company with the slogan "Feel Like a Woman, Wear a Dress!" She and her husband, Prince Egon von Furstenberg (1946–), had settled in New York City with their two young children and led a glamorous life that was well chronicled in gossip columns of the day. After a brief fashion apprenticeship, she came up with the sketch for the wrap dress. Her connections landed her an appointment with the legendary fashion editor Diana Vreeland (1901–1989) of *Vogue* magazine, and the dresses quickly caught on with the growing number of urban, middle-class professional women. At the time sales of dresses had been in decline for a few years. But the fresh, contemporary patterns on von Furstenberg's dresses lured fashion-conscious buyers, and the shirtwaist style, with a blouse top that opened down the front, seemed to flatter all body shapes.

Modern version of a wrap dress, which wraps in the front and features built-in string ties tied around the waist. *Reproduced by permission of AP/Wide World Photos.*

The dresses were practical as well: drip-dry, they required a minimum of ironing and could easily go from the office to an evening out.

Von Furstenberg's princess title and sexy looks helped make the dress a top seller by 1974, though even some of its most ardent fans complained they were becoming far too common. She built a profitable, if somewhat short-lived, fashion empire from them. In the late 1990s the original wrap dress became a prize find at vintage stores, and in 1997 von Furstenberg reintroduced a shorter version of the dress that sold for two hundred dollars.

FOR MORE INFORMATION

Brubach, Holly. "Wrap Star." *New York Times Magazine* (August 31, 1997): 51.

Diane von Furstenberg. http://www.dvf.com (accessed on August 27, 2003).

Klemesud, Judy. "Those Simple Little Dresses Seen Up and Down the Avenue." *New York Times* (November 7, 1974): 54.

Rothmeyer, Karen. "Once Upon a Time, a Princess Made It with the Hoi Polloi." *Wall Street Journal* (January 28, 1976): 1.

Headwear, 1961–79

Women's hairstyles in this period transformed from the stiff, artificial styles favored at the beginning of the 1960s to striking, short mod styles of the mid-1960s and then to the longer, loose, feathered tresses of the 1970s. Whether the styles were dramatic geometrically-shaped bob styles, longer bobs with flipped out ends, or the soft layers of the Farrah Fawcett look, the general trend in women's hairstyles was toward freer, softer styles. Hats and hair ornaments were not as important during this period, as the focus turned toward the color and styling of hair.

One of the most unique aspects of 1960s and early 1970s hairstyles was the merging of men's and women's styles. Young men and women wore styles that resembled each other. Highly fashionable young women clipped their hair short and close to their heads in the early 1960s, making them resemble boys. The styles women adopted looked very much like the bobs worn in the 1920s and passed quickly, as many fads do. But a trend toward longer hair for both men and women later in the decade brought much public comment, as many in society criticized men for growing their hair long. The longest hairstyles were worn by hippies, or young people who rejected social customs throughout the 1960s. Hippies distinguished themselves by wearing old or home-made clothes and growing their hair long. They parted their long hair in the center and left it to hang naturally over their shoulders and back. They distinguished themselves from the rest of society by rejecting established fashion trends altogether. Hippies were heavily criticized, not only for the way they looked but for their political beliefs as well, as most vigorously protested the Vietnam War (1954–75).

While the long tresses of the hippies were adopted by a relatively small group of people, longer hair had become fashionable for all by the end of the 1970s. The members of the British rock band the Beatles helped usher in a new fashion in men's hair by wearing a style called the mop top. The mop top was a messy, casual style that featured hair grown to cover men's shirt collars with full bangs that brushed the eyebrows. The mop top was a dramatic shift from the crew cuts of the previous decade. Some fashion trends limit themselves to the very wealthy or the young, but the mop top became popular for men of all ages and social classes.

Hippies often adorned their long hair with flowers and headwraps.
Reproduced by permission of © Henry Diltz/CORBIS.

Longer hair required more styling. Many men started to have their hair styled by trained stylists instead of simply cut by barbers. They began using hairdryers and special combs and brushes to achieve their desired looks. Some even had their hair set in permanent ringlet curls. By the end of the 1970s all styles of hair—long, short, straight, curly—were seen in mainstream society.

As looser styles were adopted by the majority of both men and women, an extreme style was adopted in 1976 by a group who called themselves punks. Punks were young people who identified themselves by their dramatic hairstyles, clothes, and music. Punk hairstyles were distinguished by their artificial qualities and unusual shapes. The most distinctive style was the tall mohawk. Both young female and male punks shaved the sides of their heads and left a long mohawk down the center, which they dyed a variety of colors such as bright pink or green and coated with glue to spike it out away from their heads. The stiff, artificial styles of punks inspired the creation of many new gels and hair sprays strong enough to hold long hair on end for hours.

FOR MORE INFORMATION

Corson, Richard. *Fashions in Hair: The First Five Thousand Years.* London, England: Peter Owen, 2001.

Trasko, Mary. *Daring Do's: A History of Extraordinary Hair.* New York: Flammarion, 1994.

Afro

The hairstyle of choice among African Americans from the mid-1960s through the 1970s was the Afro. The Afro featured African Americans' naturally curly hair trimmed in a full, evenly round shape around the head. During the fight for equal rights for blacks during the 1960s, as many blacks joined together to apply political pressure on the American government, they also developed their own fashion statements, which included the Afro. For many, the Afro, also known as the brush or the natural, was as much an emblem of racial pride as a fashion statement.

Many African Americans during the 1960s and 1970s wore Afros as a symbol of racial pride as well as a fashion statement. *Reproduced by permission of © Laura Doss/CORBIS.*

Prior to the 1960s most African Americans adopted straight hair, like the majority of society did, often through chemical treatments. These unnatural hairstyles fell out of favor, however, as the Civil Rights movement of the 1960s ushered in a new era of racial consciousness among American blacks. Many African Americans began to believe that allowing their hair to grow in its natural state without chemical alteration signified their acceptance of themselves and their racial identities. The Afro was a gesture of political defiance, a signal that they were ready to change the way they were treated in society. Many of the leading figures of the Civil Rights movement, including Jesse Jackson (1941–), Stokely Carmichael (1941–1998), Angela Davis (1944–), Andrew Young (1927–), and Huey Newton (1942–1989), wore the Afro hairstyle at one time or another. Over time the Afro became one of the icons of the Civil Rights movement, alongside the clenched fist salute and the slogan "Black Power."

In the 1970s the Afro grew even more popular. Popular entertainers Michael Jackson (1958–), Roberta Flack (1939–), and Richard Roundtree (1942–), and sports icons Julius Erving (1950–) and Kareem Abdul-Jabbar (1947–) lent a stylish prestige to the hairstyle, which grew ever higher and bushier. The baseball player Oscar Gamble's (1949–) luxuriant Afro grew so large that his batting helmet routinely popped off his head as he ran the bases. Beginning in the 1980s the Afro began to fall out of fashion, as a broader spectrum of African American hair and beauty styles emerged, including dreadlocks, twists, corkscrews, and fades. In the twenty-first century the classic 1970s Afro has been adopted only by trendsetters and those looking to cultivate a retro style.

FOR MORE INFORMATION

Byrd, Ayana D., and Lori Tharps. *Hair Story: Untangling the Roots of Black Hair in America.* New York: St. Martin's Press, 2001.

"Hair and Beauty Culture." *Encarta Africana.* http://www.africana.com/
archive/articles/tt_356.asp (accessed on August 27, 2003).

Farrah Fawcett Look

Charlie's Angels (1976–81), a show about the adventures of three attractive female private investigators, debuted in September 1976. By mixing sex appeal and feminist self-reliance, the series drew large audiences of both men and women, quickly becoming the top-rated television program in the United States. Former model Farrah Fawcett (1947–), then known as Farrah Fawcett-Majors, soon emerged as the most popular of the show's three stars. Her feathery blonde hair and broad white smile were the image of wholesome sensuality. Fawcett's ascent into superstardom was sealed with the release of a poster depicting her in a red swimsuit. It sold some eight million copies and was a fixture on the bedroom walls of American teenage boys from coast to coast.

Farrah Fawcett-Majors's feathered tresses were all the rage in the late 1970s. *Reproduced by permission of AP/Wide World Photos.*

Fawcett's hairstyle in particular seemed to touch a nerve with the public. Before long, young girls and women across the nation began to adopt the Farrah Fawcett look, a flipped back, winged, layered and tousled style held in place with plentiful amounts of gel and spray. "Farrahmania" reached its peak in 1977. At one point a Farrah-mad entrepreneur reportedly offered five million dollars to bottle water from the starlet's kitchen tap. She declined. As Fawcett's acting career fizzled, so did her influence on fashion. The feathered Farrah Fawcett look dropped from fashion in the early 1980s. The style was revived in the late 1990s, when designers started to couple the hairstyle with 1980s-inspired apparel. Singers Madonna (1958–) and Gwen Stefani (1969–), country music phenom LeAnn Rimes (1982–), rapper Mary J. Blige (c. 1971–), and actresses Liv Tyler (1977–), Jenna Elfman (1971–), and Pamela Anderson (1967–) all adopted the cut in the early twenty-first century.

FOR MORE INFORMATION

Burstein, Patricia. *Farrah: An Unauthorized Biography of Farrah Fawcett-Majors.* New York: New American Library, 1977.

Oliva, Christine. "Feathered Hair on the Cutting Edge." *Cincinnati Enquirer* (July 6, 2000).

The Flip

The Flip was a bouncy, upturned hairdo that was widely worn by young women throughout the 1960s. Its name derived from a flip, or upturned curl at the ends. Starting out as a modified version of the bouffant, its stiffness relaxed over the decade along with hairstyle trends in general. By the early 1970s it had given way to a longer, looser version.

Television actress Mary Tyler Moore (1936–) wore a short version of the Flip when *The Dick Van Dyke Show* debuted in 1961. Moore played Laura Petrie, an endearing housewife who was married to a television writer. The show focused on the Petries' home life in suburban New York City, and Moore wore cropped pants known as capris on the show, often with flat shoes. This was a marked change from other television wives, who seemed to go about their day in impractical swishy dresses, high heels, and upswept hair. Moore's comedic talents on the hit show won her two Emmy Awards, and her chin-length Flip hairstyle was widely copied. A version with bangs became especially popular. Requiring just a light setting lotion and curlers, the Flip typified an energetic, no-fuss American style.

In 1966 a new television show debuted with another dark-haired actress whose Flip hairstyle was also emulated: *That Girl* (1966–71). The sitcom starred Marlo Thomas (1943–) as an aspiring actress and single young woman in New York City. Her stylish designer outfits, including miniskirts, helped make Thomas's perky character a fashion icon. Her Flip hairstyle fell to shoulder-length and beyond, moving with a trend toward longer hair. The looser style reflected a new emphasis on haircutting techniques over elaborate salon styling methods.

FOR MORE INFORMATION

Gladfelter, Elizabeth. "Marlo Thomas: Beyond That Flip." *WWD* (August 7, 1997): S6.

"The Hair That's in Fashion." *Vogue* (January 1963): 96–97.

Geometric Bob Styles

English hairdresser Vidal Sassoon (1928–) established the first of what would become a successful chain of hair salons on London's Bond Street in 1954. Over the next few years he gained a reputation for creating daring but flattering looks for a stylish clientele. His work began appearing in the top fashion magazines of the day. In the early 1960s, however, women's hairstyles were elaborate, stiffened sculptures. They required setting lotion, rollers, dryer time, backcombing, and a generous amount of hair spray. Sassoon railed against such styles as out of step with the modern woman's lifestyle. In 1963 actress Nancy Kwan (1939–) was brought to Sassoon's salon during the shooting of a film called *The Wild Affair* (1963). Kwan had very long hair, and filmmakers wanted it cut. Sassoon created an uneven, layered cut inspired, he said, by architecture. The finished effect was so dramatic that he called a fashion photographer immediately, and Kwan's profile was shot that same day for the British and American editions of *Vogue* magazine. A year later Sassoon gave model Grace Coddington (c. 1923–) his Five Point Cut on the night before she appeared in designer Mary Quant's (1934–) fashion show. Sassoon's Five Point Cut featured five inverted "V"s designed to highlight a woman's eyes, cheekbones, and neck.

The short, modern haircuts, which swung when their bearers danced, belonged to the same spirit as Quant's miniskirts.

Originating in London with the mod style and with new rock groups like the Beatles, whose famous mop-top hair Sassoon also cut, this new focus on youthful playfulness rejected many of the conventions of the sedate 1950s: women's clothes were designed to accentuate a slim, boyish shape, and Sassoon's almost genderless hairstyle needed a minimum of styling and upkeep. He opened a New York City salon in 1965, followed by others in California.

FOR MORE INFORMATION

Montgomery, Christine. "Sassoon Style." *Washington Times* (October 16, 1997): 10.

"Sassoon and His Scissors." *Life* (July 9, 1965): 67–68.

Sassoon, Vidal. "Forever Cutting Edge." *Vogue* (April 2002): 90.

Long Hair for Men

Perhaps no modern fashion trend has been as controversial as that of men growing their hair long. Beginning with the beatniks and hippies—names given to those who rejected the established customs of society in the 1950s and 1960s—and spreading quickly throughout society, long hair on men represented a rebellion against the clean-cut image that had prevailed during previous decades. Hippies often wore their hair down to their shoulders and longer as a sign of protest against American involvement in the Vietnam War (1954–75) and to set themselves apart from the mainstream society. The popular Broadway musical *Hair* (1968) dramatized the importance of long hair to the anticonformist feelings of the youth of the 1960s. Jeff Poniewaz's poem "Why Young Men Wore Their Hair Long in the Sixties" in *Viet Nam Generation* illustrates the principals that many men felt lay behind their decision to grow their hair: "Because the first thing they do in / a prison an insane asylum or the Marines / is shear off all your hair exactly like sheep."

Many people, especially older people, saw the increasing length of men's hair as a challenge to the conservative values of patriotism, religion, and masculinity. Some people got aggressively angry and threatened or attacked men with long hair. Many schools and businesses made rules about the acceptable length of men's and boys'

hair. Even governments had opinions on the subject. Greek dictator George Papadopoulos (1919–1999) banned long hair on men
in 1967 as a part of his repressive military government.

As the political significance of long hair faded after the 1960s
and 1970s, the acceptable length for men's hair became much more
flexible and long hair passed from political statement to fashion statement. By the twenty-first century men were able to wear their hair
in a variety of different lengths, from shaved bald to below the shoulders. Still, long hair retained some symbolic resistance to dominant
cultural styles.

Many saw the 1960s trend of long hair on men as a rebellion against the conformity and conservative values embraced by those who favored crew cuts. *Reproduced by permission of © Lynn Goldsmith/CORBIS.*

FOR MORE INFORMATION

Brown, Joe David. *The Hippies*. Richmond, VA: Time, 1967.

Poniewaz, Jeff. "Why Young Men Wore Their Hair Long in the Sixties."
Viet Nam Generation (March 1994).

Simpson, T. "Real Men, Short Hair." *Intellectual Digest* (November 1973):
76–78.

Body Decorations, 1961–79

People adorned their bodies in widely varying ways in the 1960s and 1970s. The popularity of modern styles at the beginning of the 1960s brought huge plastic flower ornaments, heavy makeup, especially around the eyes, and false eyelashes for women. Men accepted jewelry as part of their wardrobe, starting with the love beads hung around their necks in the 1960s and ending the period with multiple chains of gold adorning their necks and chests, bracelets around their wrists, and rings on their fingers.

The middle years of this time period were punctuated by the antifashion of the hippies, or people who rejected society's conventional customs and embraced free personal expression. Although hippies were relatively few in number, they brought natural, homemade adornment and political symbols into the limelight. Both men and women tucked real flowers behind their ears and wore homemade jewelry. Many wore strings of love beads around their necks, peace symbols, and buttons protesting the

Body piercing is an ancient practice that has become fashionable with young people as a way to express one's individuality. *Reproduced by permission of © Jim Cornfield/CORBIS.*

PUNK

Punk was a radical style of the mid- to late 1970s marked by unconventional combinations of elements and materials and a high shock value. It emerged out of London, England, and New York, feeding off of the cities' angry, rebellious participants of music concerts where a new type of music called punk was developing. What began as an antistyle aimed at thumbing its nose at the established norms of high fashion ended up having a great deal of influence on the fashions of the late 1970s and beyond.

There was always a punk element in rock 'n' roll. The Beatles famously wore black leather jackets and played a loud, fast, aggressive brand of rock music before softening their look and sound. What is now called punk is generally dated to 1972, however, when the British fashion designers Malcolm McLaren (1946–) and Vivienne Westwood (1941–) opened their London boutique. First called Too Fast To Live, Too Young To Die and later renamed Sex, the shop sold a variety of black leather and rubber designs and became a central meeting place for those in the emerging punk music scene. An aspiring music manager, McLaren himself helped set the styles that many British punks would emulate. Some of these he imported from the United

States. From the U.S. punk musician Richard Hell of the band Television, for example, McLaren copied the idea of the spiked haircut. Achieved by applying large amounts of gel or Vaseline to one's hair and then rubbing talcum powder into it to dry it into spikes that stuck out away from the head, the hairstyle became emblematic of the punk look. Johnny Rotten (1956–), lead singer of the band McLaren managed, the Sex Pistols, helped popularize the style in Great Britain. Other early elements of punk style that migrated from the United States to England included the concept of deliberately ripping one's jeans below the knee, a practice of the New York-based bands the Ramones and the New York Dolls.

In contrast to the colorful, naturalistic garments worn by the hippies of the 1960s, punks preferred almost entirely black, self-consciously menacing clothes. They often composed their outfits little by little from items bought at second-hand or military surplus shops, mixing, matching, and layering as they saw fit. Quite often the garments were torn, colored, or otherwise altered to create a more individual look. Mainstays of the punk's closet included black turtlenecks, short leather skirts for women, tight leather pants or jeans for men, leather jackets customized with paint, chains, and metal studs, and Doc Marten boots. Jackets and T-shirts were often decorated with ob-

Vietnam War (1954–75) to signal their desire for peace. Hippies also made Native American jewelry and headbands fashionable for whites to wear.

After the Vietnam War ended, fashion shifted again toward artificial, flamboyant styles. The gaudiest styles were developed by dancers at discotheques, or bars where people gathered to dance to music, and punks, who created a deliberately aggressive style of dress. Disco style was glamorous, with glittery jewelry and colored glasses complementing the bold clothes. Punk style was the opposite. Punks stuck safety pins through their skin, wore heavy metal chains and spiky dog collars around their necks, and

scene or disturbing words and images. Besides leather, materials favored by punks included rubber and plastic; besides chains, they liked to adorn themselves with dog collars, razor blades, and safety pins which became a symbol of the punk style.

Punks also blazed their own trails in the area of hair, makeup, and jewelry. When not spiking hair, they were coloring it in a variety of bright hues. Or they shaved part or all of their heads, creating mohawks. Makeup was used to blacken eyelids and lips. Finally, the most dedicated punks pierced their cheeks, noses, and eyelids, often with safety pins.

Punk remained a rebellious style until 1977, when designer Zandra Rhodes (1940–) brought it into the high fashion mainstream with her Punk Chic collection. Her designs offered a tamer version of punk style, including tattered hems with exquisite embroidery and gold safety pins. Her designs helped bring punk to the attention of the rich and famous and paved the way for its acceptance by the mass market. By the end of the 1970s, new wave—a tidier, less threatening variation of punk—had largely replaced it as the style of choice among New York and London youth. However, the punk spirit proved a major influence on the goth, grunge, and some hip-hop styles of subsequent decades.

Punks of the 1970s often spiked their hair into mohawks. *Reproduced by permission of Susan D. Rock.*

painted themselves with black eye makeup, fingernail polish, and lipstick.

FOR MORE INFORMATION

Schoeffler, O. E., and William Gale. *Esquire's Encyclopedia of 20th Century Men's Fashions.* New York: McGraw-Hill, 1973.

Steele, Valerie. *Fifty Years of Fashion: New Look to Now.* New Haven, CT: Yale University Press, 1997.

Body Piercing

Body piercing involves making a hole in a body part and, usually, placing a piece of jewelry into the hole. Body piercing is often defined as the piercing of any body part for men and the piercing of any part besides the earlobes for women, for whom pierced ears have long been acceptable. An ancient practice, body piercing has been done in many cultures for reasons of adornment or ritual. Though it first became popular in modern times in the punk culture of the 1970s and 1980s, which rose up alongside punk rock music, body piercing later became surprisingly popular with many more mainstream young people.

Prehistoric art has shown that piercing body parts occurred long before recorded civilization. The pharaohs of ancient Egypt often pierced their navels, and Roman soldiers were known to prove their masculinity and bravery by piercing their nipples. Among African and Native American peoples, ritual piercings were often part of religious or coming-of-age ceremonies. Enduring painful piercings has been a proof of courage and a symbol of identity in many cultures.

The rebellious youth of the 1970s and 1980s found shocking ways to assert their identities. Punks wore shredded clothing and dyed their hair bright colors and shaved and shaped it into spikes and ridges such as the Mohawk (a ridge of hair sticking straight up, running down the center of the head). They got tattoos and pierced their bodies in many places rarely seen in modern Western culture, performing many of the piercings themselves. It was typical to see punk youth wearing safety pins in their pierced ears, noses, eyebrows, and cheeks.

If the early punk piercings were all about rebellion and shock, later piercings had a more fashionable purpose. The ears were still a popular spot to pierce, but instead of one earring now each ear might hold a number of earrings, ranging from the lobe to the top of the ear. Noses, eyebrows, lips, and tongues were also frequent locations for jewelry, and some people pierced their nipples and navel. Pierced genitals were not uncommon but generally were only for the most extreme fans of piercing. Celebrities from sports stars like Dennis Rodman (1961–) to pop singers like Janet Jackson

(1966–) pierced their nose, tongue, and navel. Young people from adolescents to college athletes began to imitate them, with many viewing tongue and eyebrow piercing as cool, sexy, and socially acceptable.

FOR MORE INFORMATION

Gay, Kathlyn. *Body Marks: Tattooing, Piercing, and Scarification.* Brookfield, CT: Millbrook Press, 2002.

Graves, Bonnie B. *Tattooing and Body Piercing.* Mankato, MN: Life Matters, 2000.

Wójcik, Daniel. *Punk and Neo-Tribal Body Art.* Jackson, MS: University Press of Mississippi, 1995.

[*See also* **Volume 5, 1980–2003: Tattooing**]

Mood Rings

The mood ring was one of the biggest fashion fads of the 1970s. Marketed as an accessory for the "Me Decade," a time when people began to actively explore their feelings, the color-changing jewelry first became popular in New York City and quickly spread throughout the United States. Each mood ring contained a temperature-sensitive liquid crystal encased in quartz. As the body temperature of the wearer changed, the crystals changed colors. Each color the ring displayed supposedly corresponded to a different mood. There were seven colors in all, each with a different meaning: blue meant happy; reddish brown meant insecure; black meant the wearer was upset; golden yellow was a sign of tension; and so on. From a scientific perspective the mood ring did have some validity as an indicator of someone's emotional state; the metal band of a mood ring conducted heat from the finger to the liquid crystal, which changed color in response to the temperature of the skin.

The mood ring was invented in 1975 by Joshua Reynolds, a thirty-three-year-old marketing executive from New York City who took an incredibly simple product idea and turned it into a

One of the most popular fads of the 1970s, the mood ring supposedly kept people in touch with their feelings. *Photograph by Dan Newell. Reproduced by permission of Leitha Etheridge-Sims.*

national craze. After making a fortune off the mood ring, Reynolds later went on to invent the ThighMaster exercise machine.

Like all fads the mood ring had a very limited life span. In this case the life span of the product was quite literally fixed, in that the heat-sensitive crystals would only emit their color changes for a period of two years before they would settle permanently into a shade of black. By 1977, just two years after their introduction, the rings had faded in popularity.

FOR MORE INFORMATION

Long, Mark A. *Bad Fads.* Toronto, Canada: ECW Press, 2002.

Neckties

A decorative piece of fabric knotted around the neck has been a part of the clothing of Western men since the seventeenth century, though the exact nature of the necktie has changed frequently over that time. Neckties have been wide or narrow, brightly patterned or somber, depending on the current rules of fashion. Because business clothes for men have remained rather conservative throughout the twentieth century, the necktie was often the only piece of clothing through which a man could express his individuality. Women have also worn neckties as part of a tailored look. Women's neckties became particularly popular in the late 1970s, inspired by actress Diane Keaton's offbeat style in Woody Allen's movie *Annie Hall* (1977). However, neckties have predominantly been required formalwear for men.

When the tie, then called a cravat, got its start around 1650, it developed from simple, loosely tied pieces of fabric into elaborate lacy scarves that tied in back or were knotted in a bow at the neck. By the mid-1800s, however, men's neckwear became simpler. The lacy cravat was abandoned and most men wore a necktie held in place by a stickpin, or a bow tie, also called a butterfly tie. Though the early 1900s would see a short period of popularity for the English ascot, a wide scarf that tied loosely under the chin, for the most part the simple straight necktie and the bow tie would remain the standard choices for men's neckwear during the twentieth century.

Some social commentators insist, with some humor, that necktie styles can predict the state of the economy. When ties are wide and flashy, they say economic times will be hard, such as in the 1930s, a time of economic depression, when neckties were worn as much as four inches wide. Narrow and conservative ties, such as the ones worn in the booming economy of the 1950s, however, predict a healthy economy.

Whether an economic indicator or not, the changes in men's tie styles certainly indicate the social climate of the times. During the flashy 1970s, designer Ralph Lauren (1939–) introduced ties that were five inches wide and brightly colored. The conservative 1980s saw the arrival of the "power tie" in yellow or red, which, worn with a dark suit, represented the high-powered dealmakers of the time. By the 1990s the power politics of the 1980s had become identified with greed and ruthlessness, and power ties lost their appeal. No matter the time period ties have been used to express male individuality.

FOR MORE INFORMATION

Gibbings, Sarah. *The Tie: Trends and Traditions.* Washington, DC: Barron's, 1990.

Gross, Kim Johnson. *Shirt and Tie.* New York: Alfred Knopf, 1993.

[*See also* **Volume 3, Seventeenth Century: Cravats; Volume 3, Eighteenth Century: Jabot; Volume 3, Nineteenth Century: Ascots**]

Puka Chokers

Strings of white puka shell beads emerged as a teen fashion trend in the early 1970s. Puka shells are the leftover parts from the shell of the cone snail found on beaches in Hawaii. The empty conical shells, closed at the larger end, are swept back into the surf. In

Strings of puka shells being sold as souvenirs in Hawaii. Traditional garb for Hawaiians, the shells were worn by surfers in the 1960s and fashion trendsetters in the 1970s. *Reproduced by permission of © Tim Thompson/CORBIS.*

the waves they then break apart into the flat, jagged white pieces that make up the puka shell choker. Calcium deposits leave a tiny hole, known as a *puka* in Hawaiian, in the center, through which they can be threaded. They were part of traditional Hawaiian dress for centuries and were adopted by surfers in the 1960s. The actual shells range from shades of white to blue, brown, or purple, but much of the 1970s puka craze involved pure white shells, which were often imitations of the real shells. Actress Elizabeth Taylor (1932–) wore puka shells and was reportedly bombarded with questions about them. Actor and singer David Cassidy (1950–) went to Hawaii for a vacation and the craze began when he appeared on *The Partridge Family* wearing the shells. Both Cassidy and the sitcom about a family rock band were massive hits, and his trendy wardrobe and shaggy haircut were widely copied.

By 1974 the puka choker fad was even mentioned in respected news magazine *Newsweek*. Many of the puka chokers sold in stores in the United States were fake shells, but the more expensive, genuine puka chokers were being sold in Beverly Hills, California, boutiques like the one owned by Priscilla Presley (1945–), ex-wife of rock star Elvis Presley (1935–1977), for up to $150. Tourists in Hawaii combed the beaches for the shells, which were difficult to find, to make their own necklaces. In the late 1990s puka chokers enjoyed a brief revival among teens with a fondness for surf styles.

FOR MORE INFORMATION

Axthelm, Pete. "Puka, Puka, Who's Got the Puka?" *Newsweek* (September 9, 1974): 49.

Rubin, Sylvia. "Trendspotting." *San Francisco Chronicle* (July 15, 2001): 6.

Tanning

One of the primary reasons why travelers who live in northern climates head off to fair-weather vacation spots is to smooth on suntan lotion, pass hours soaking in sunshine, and emerge with their skin browned by the sun's ultraviolet (UV) rays. Not everyone who desires tanned skin has the time or inclination to stay in the sun for the time needed to obtain brown skin. As a result, artificial means

Though a tan is seen as an outward expression of good health, excessive exposure to sunlight—natural or artificial—can cause skin cancer. *Reproduced by permission of © Royalty-Free/ CORBIS.*

have been devised to tan skin even during the coldest and bleakest weather.

Sunlamps are the primary non-natural method of acquiring a tan. A sunlamp is a source of light that generates UV rays, resulting in an artificially produced but natural-looking tan. Some sunlamps feature adjustable lamp heads that can be pointed at any angle, so that the user can focus the light on a specific body part. Smaller lamps are specifically designed as facial tanners.

Sunlamps became fashionable during the 1960s, when beach culture was popularized in the California-oriented songs of such rock groups as the Beach Boys and Jan and Dean and on screen in such teen-oriented movies as *Beach Party* (1963), *Muscle Beach Party* (1964), *Bikini Beach* (1964), and *Beach Blanket Bingo* (1965). Teens and young adults wished to look as tan and attractive as Frankie Avalon (1940–) and Annette Funicello (1942–), the popular stars of the *Beach Party* films. If they did not live in warm climates and have daily access to the sun, they could purchase sunlamps and tan themselves indoors. During the 1960s artificial tanning creams also became available. Such products as Rapid Tan, QT (Quick Tan), Tan-O-Rama, and Man-Tan featured dihydroxyacetone, a colorless substance that turned the skin dark brown. The downside to such products was that they irritated the skin and stained clothing, and the tans they produced often were uneven or blotchy.

In the 1970s and 1980s more and more Americans became concerned with feeling fit and looking good and, as a result, indoor tanning salons opened up across the country. Tanning salons were businesses that featured tanning beds, located in separate booths or rooms to insure privacy. Customers relaxed on the clamshell-shaped beds, while their bodies were exposed to the artificial sunlight generated by the tubular bulbs that surrounded them. Booths were equipped with timers to prevent overexposure to the light. At this time tanned skin became so associated with physical fitness and vigor that tanning beds and sun lamps even were featured in health clubs, which primarily existed to allow their members to lift weights, run on treadmills, ride stationary bicycles, or play tennis.

Tanned skin had developed a reputation as a signal of health, but by the mid-1970s that idea had started to be challenged. Scientists discovered that although exposure to sunlight or the artificial light produced by sunlamps may allow the body to manufacture Vitamin D, which plays a primary role in building bones and teeth, only a tiny quantity of light is required for all the Vitamin D the body needs. Scientists also determined that even a moderate amount of the UV radiation that causes the skin to darken also harms the body's immune system. Exposure to UV rays has been linked to the early aging of skin, causing it to look rough and leathery and, more seriously, can cause malignant melanoma, a deadly skin cancer. The negative effects of tanning often are not immediately apparent. Young people in their teens or twenties may not suffer the ill-effects of tanned skin until middle or old age.

Despite these health concerns, tanning salons remain popular. In the early twenty-first century over 28,000 tanning salons were open for business across the United States. Additionally, relaxing and playing in the sun continue to be favorite pastimes, and beach resorts remain popular vacation destinations.

FOR MORE INFORMATION

Sweet, Cheryl A. *"Healthy Tan"—A Fast-Fading Myth.* Rockville, MD: Department of Health and Human Services, Public Health Service, Food and Drug Administration, 1990.

Waud, Sydney P. *Sunbathing: The Healthy Way to a Perfect Tan.* New York: Mayflower Books, 1979.

Footwear, 1961–79

The footwear styles available in the 1960s and 1970s offered men and women a wide range of choices in heel height, material, color, and design. Some footwear styles were considered ultrafashionable. Among these were go-go boots and feminine styles of shoes, similar to those from the 1920s, which were worn by young women in miniskirts in the 1960s. Fashionable men wore white slip-on shoes or low ankle boots with side elastic or zippers. These styles were available in leather but also in new, soft leather substitutes and other man-made materials. Footwear came dyed in a variety of different colors and was often treated with a glossy finish that made shoes look wet. Similar fads for platform shoes and shiny patent leather and plastic shoes emerged during this time.

Other footwear styles were considered antifashion, including the earth shoes and Birkenstocks worn by people concerned with following healthful, natural lifestyles and the Doc Martens worn first by rebellious British youth known as skinheads and soon by other youths throughout Europe and the United States. In addition to these styles a fad for exercise started a trend toward wearing tennis shoes and specialized running shoes by people of all walks of life. By the 1970s even more varieties of shoe styles came onto the market. People could wear anything from classically styled pumps and oxfords to platform styles in neon shades to sturdier, practical sport shoes.

FOR MORE INFORMATION

Lawlor, Laurie. *Where Will This Shoe Take You?: A Walk Through the History of Footwear.* New York: Walker and Co., 1996.

Pratt, Lucy, and Linda Woolley. *Shoes.* London, England: V&A Publications, 1999.

Footwear of the 1960s and 1970s was as varied as the clothing worn with it. *Reproduced by permission of © Bettmann/ CORBIS.*

Birkenstocks

Birkenstock sandals are specially designed casual shoes with flexible cork and latex (type of rubber) insoles that are shaped like the bottom of a person's foot. Designed in Germany, Birkenstocks were first introduced in the United States in the late 1960s, and they immediately became identified with a youthful generation who preferred natural and comfortable clothing to the more restrictive fashions of their parents. Birkenstocks introduced the concept of "comfort shoes" that has been continued by many other manufacturers.

Karl Birkenstock came from a family of German shoemakers. His grandfather Konrad had first come up with the idea that shoes would be more comfortable if the soles were contoured or shaped like the bottom of a foot. In 1897 he invented a flexible insole that fit inside a shoe to increase its comfort, and he sold his insoles successfully all over Germany and Europe. In 1964 his grandson Karl invented a shoe that used Konrad's idea by making a cork sole that was shaped like a footprint.

In 1966 Margot Fraser, a German woman who had moved to the United States, visited her native country where she tried Birkenstock's sandals. She found them to be the most comfortable shoes she had ever worn, ending the foot pain she had experienced for years. She brought them back to the United States and began to sell them from her home. She tried to sell them to shoe stores, but the managers of the stores took one look at the boxy, plain Birkenstocks and laughed at her. They told her that American women would never buy shoes that looked like that.

Fraser then decided to approach people who might have less conventional ideas. As a result, she began to sell her shoes at health food stores, which were popular among a small, but growing, number of people at the time. Birkenstocks became so popular during the late 1960s and 1970s that specialty shoe stores began to sell them, too. During the conservative 1980s the shoes went out of fashion somewhat, but by the 1990s they had come back more successfully than ever. By the early twenty-first century many styles of Birkenstocks had been designed, including hiking boots and men's and women's formal shoes. Birkenstock sandals were even seen on

Birkenstock sandals, with their flexible cork and latex insoles, were designed as the ultimate comfort shoe. *Reproduced by permission of Birkenstock.*

the runways at designer fashion shows. The basic footprint design has remained unchanged throughout the years, as has the company's commitment to comfort over fashion.

Though thousands of people buy and wear Birkenstocks, they are still very much seen as the shoes of social rebels or political radicals, and people often assume they know the political beliefs of those who wear them. In fact "Birkenstock-wearing" is an adjective regularly used to describe environmental activists or those who support other social causes, usually by those who disagree with them. In reality, however, all types of people have found comfort in the Birkenstock sandal. Margot Fraser's company, Birkenstock Footprint Sandal, Inc., lives up to the shoe's liberal, open-minded image, supporting recycling, Earth Day, and other environmental causes. Refusing many offers to sell out, the California-based company is moving toward becoming totally worker owned.

FOR MORE INFORMATION

Birkenstock. http://www.birkenstock.com (accessed on August 27, 2003).

Brokaw, Leslie. "Feet Don't Fail Me Now." *Inc* (May 1994): 70–76.

Doc Martens

Though Dr. Martens Air Wair is the brand name of many different styles of shoes, many people only mean one thing when they speak of Doc Martens: thick soled, black leather work boots that have been favored by rebellious youth internationally since the 1960s. First produced as a corrective shoe for people with foot problems, and later marketed as a work boot for people whose jobs kept them on their feet all day, tough-looking Doc Martens have been the boot of choice for many different youth movements.

After the end of World War II (1939–45), a German doctor named Klaus Maertens injured his foot while skiing in the European Alps. Seeking a comfortable shoe for his recovery, he joined with German engineer Herbert Funck to design a special sole of rubber sealed around pockets of air. The first air-cushioned soles were made from army surplus tires. Dr. Maertens's shoes were first popular among older people throughout Germany who wanted comfortable, sturdy shoes. Maertens thought his shoes could sell successfully in other countries, too. In the late 1950s respected British shoe manufacturer R. Griggs and Company bought the rights to Maertens's special air-cushioned sole and designed sturdy work boots and shoes that used it. They changed the name to Dr. Martens, thinking that the German spelling of the name would harm sales in post–World War II Europe where anti-German sentiment remained high due to the millions of people killed during the war when Germany invaded several European countries.

The first Dr. Martens work boot, made of black leather with distinctive yellow stitching around the sole, came off the assembly line on April 1, 1960 (the style is called 1460 after the European style of marking the date: day, month, year). Though the manufacturers intended 1460s to be used by police and fire fighters, they were soon adopted by people in their teens and twenties, first throughout Britain, then internationally.

During the 1960s many young working-class Brits who felt little connection with mainstream society became skinheads. Skinhead was the name given to young people who shaved their heads and dressed in military clothes, black leather, or other threatening kinds of clothing, for a variety of political reasons. Some were racist white supremacists, while others held quite opposite antiracist views. In the suburbs and wealthier classes, many people adopted elements of skinhead style as a fashion. For the skinheads and their imitators, big, black, clunky Doc Martens, or Docs, as they are sometimes called, were the perfect footwear because they looked threatening and tough.

In the 1970s many gays and lesbians joined the ranks of young people wearing Doc Martens, perhaps feeling the heavy boots gave them the strength to survive the hatred and prejudice directed at them. During the 1980s rebellious youth groups called punks and goths rejected mainstream culture and dressed in outlandish styles, often dyeing their hair and piercing body parts. Punks and goths made Doc Martens their own by painting them and piercing them with safety pins. In the 1990s Docs became part of the uniform of the laid-back grunge lifestyle. The identification of Doc Martens with rebellion caused some schools to ban them.

Having gone from work boots to a radical extreme, Doc Martens had, by the late 1990s, become fashion shoes, made in many styles. Famous people from singer Elton John (1947–) to religious leader the Dalai Lama (1935–) to film character Harry Potter have worn them, and the Pope liked them so much he ordered one hundred pairs in white for his staff. In the mid-1990s Doc Martens was rated among the thirty best-known brands in the world.

FOR MORE INFORMATION

Dr. Martens Air Wair. http://www.drmartens.com (accessed on August 27, 2003).

"Great British Brands: Dr. Martens." *Marketing* (August 1, 2002): 19.

Earth Shoes

In the late 1960s and early 1970s, young people began dressing less formally. Even footwear became more casual, as girls and women shunned high heels and boys and men avoided dress shoes even for formal occasions. Out of this desire for attire that was more comfortable came the advent of the earth shoe: footwear, often made of soft tanned leather, which featured a heel that was positioned lower than the toes. This design was said to align the body so that the pelvis and shoulders naturally swayed back, enhancing posture and permitting deeper, improved breathing.

Earth shoes were created for men and women, often handsewn, and came in various styles. They were designed as a traditional shoe but with as few as two or as many as eight pairs of holes for laces. They sometimes were backless and were fastened by buckles or straps instead of laces. They came as boots, high-tops, and even sandals. Whatever their style, they stretched and bended with the shape and movement of the foot. They were touted as ideal walking shoes.

The first earth shoes were designed in the 1950s and 1960s by Anne Kalso, a Danish yoga instructor. (Yoga is a type of exercise that enhances both the mind and the body.) Supposedly earth shoes were first commercially sold in the United States on April 22, 1970, the very first Earth Day, a yearly observance that spotlights the importance of environmental conservation. This explains how they came to be called earth shoes, which even became one of the popular brand names for this style of footwear.

FOR MORE INFORMATION

Lawlor, Laurie. *Where Will This Shoe Take You?: A Walk Through the History of Footwear.* New York: Walker and Co., 1996.

Yue, Charlotte, and David Yue. *Shoes: Their History in Words and Pictures.* Boston, MA: Houghton Mifflin, 1997.

Go-Go Boots

In the swinging mid-1960s a stylish young woman would never be caught on a discotheque dance floor without her go-go boots: bold, white, or candy-colored vinyl or leather boots of various heights. Usually worn with miniskirts or dresses, go-go boots were pulled on, laced up, or zippered up, and featured a wide range of heels. The height of the leg-hugging boot was determined by the length of the skirt to be worn with it. Often the shorter the skirt was, the taller the accompanying boot.

The term "go-go boots" emerged from the popularity of discotheques. The first American discotheque was the Whisky a Go-Go, which opened in Hollywood, California, in 1963. At Whisky a Go-Go young women wearing miniskirts danced on platforms or in cages suspended high above the dance floor. They were called go-go dancers. Soon young women across the nation started to dress like them. French designer André Courreges (1923–) introduced what would become go-go boots in 1964. His white ankle-high boot featured a square toe and low, square heel and was worn with dresses hemmed three inches above the knee. It was not long until go-go dancers

The rule of thumb for wearing go-go boots: the shorter the skirt, the taller the boot. *Reproduced by permission of © H. Armstrong Roberts/CORBIS.*

and then other fashionable young women were clad in variations of the Courreges boot.

Nancy Sinatra (1940–), the singer-daughter of celebrated singer-actor Frank Sinatra (1915–1998), was the queen of go-go boots. Her 1965 pop hit, "These Boots Are Made for Walkin'," sold just under four million copies. Photographs and record album covers from the 1960s feature Sinatra wearing white go-go boots and matching white minidress, brown boots accompanying a daring, hip-hugging sweater, and an ensemble of red boots and matching red minidress.

Go-go boots, like go-go dancers, were just a fad. Despite the success of Sinatra's song in 1965, that same year the go-go boot lost its fashion appeal. However, variations of go-go boots remained a part of young women's wardrobes into the 1970s.

FOR MORE INFORMATION

Beard, Tyler. *Art of the Boot.* Salt Lake City, UT: Gibbs Smith Publishers, 1999.

Patent Leather Shoes

In 1818 creative New Jersey inventor Seth Boyden (1788–1870) discovered a special finishing process during which several layers of dyes, oils, varnishes, or resins were applied to unfinished leather, giving it a hard, glossy finish. Shoe factories near his home in Newark soon began producing fashionable shoes from the new leather. By the end of the nineteenth century young boys and girls of wealthy families wore black patent leather slippers, and they were also a popular choice for adult formal wear. In the 1920s a popular men's hairstyle where the hair was slicked down flat with oil was known as the patent leather look.

Patent leather saw a surge in popularity during the 1950s and 1960s, when it was used for young girls' formal shoes. Following the difficulties of World War II (1939–45), the 1950s and early 1960s were booming economic times. The introduction of television and many new electric appliances were part of a general atmosphere that valued things that were modern, shiny, and new. Glossy black, and sometimes white, patent leather shoes were a standard part of the wardrobe of girls from all classes and ethnic backgrounds, to be worn for special occasions or to places of worship. In fact, one of the most enduring popular stories about patent leather shoes comes from a religious source. It is commonly reported by those who grew up during the 1960s that Roman Catholic priests and nuns warned girls away from patent leather, telling them that the glossy surface of the shoes would reflect their underpants. This bit of folklore, whether true or not, has led to many popular jokes and at least one theatrical production, Bill McHale's 1985 musical play *Do Patent Leather Shoes Really Reflect Up?*, a humorous examination of a Catholic childhood.

Toward the end of the twentieth century dress became more casual, and patent leather shoes were no longer a required part of a young girl's wardrobe. They are still worn by children and adults as formal shoes, however, and 2001 saw a modern twist on the classic leather when the shoe manufacturer Nike introduced "retro" Air Jordan patent leather sneakers, selling for $125.

FOR MORE INFORMATION

Pratt, Lucy, and Linda Woolley. *Shoes.* London: V&A, 1999.

Yue, Charlotte, and David Yue. *Shoes: Their History in Words and Pictures.* Boston, MA: Houghton Mifflin, 1997.

Platform Shoes

Platforms are shoes with heavy soles that can range from half-an-inch to six-inches thick and made their first memorable appearance during the 1600s, when shoes with high platform soles called chopines were popular among wealthy women in Venice, Italy. During the 1930s cork-soled shoes with wedge-shaped platform soles became popular among many women, but these shoes were fairly conservative, usually having a platform of an inch or less.

During the 1960s rebellious youth began to wear ragged thrift shop and homemade clothes, which evolved into a very col-

Platform shoes were considered a symbol of 1970s excess in dress. *Reproduced by permission of © Gary Houlder/CORBIS.*

orful, flamboyant fashion. Clothing manufacturers had caught up with youthful trends and had begun making stylish, flashy clothes by the end of the decade. Wide-leg bell-bottom pants and short skirts were worn with platform shoes, often several inches tall. The platforms of the 1970s were very high, often brightly colored, and made of shiny material or plastic, and, for the first time, both women and men wore them. The new shoes were seen on such popular American rock stars as the members of KISS and British singer Elton John (1947–), as well as in the successful 1977 disco film *Saturday Night Fever.*

While the new tall platform shoes may have looked good on the disco dance floor, they were not always easy to dance in. Doctors began to call them "ankle busters," because they treated so many injuries caused by platforms. Once they went out of style, many were sure that the impractical shoe would never return. However, after the conservative 1980s came to an end, many people had fond feelings for the styles of the 1970s, and platform shoes came back into fashion by the mid-1990s. In the early twenty-first century some young Japanese women adopted a style that included spiked hair, miniskirts, and tall platform shoes.

FOR MORE INFORMATION

Ellsworth, Ray. *Platform Shoes: A Big Step in Fashion.* Atglen, PA: Schiffer Publishing, 1998.

[*See also* **Volume 3, Sixteenth Century: Chopines**]

Tennis Shoes

The first tennis shoe, called the plimsoll, was a rubber-soled canvas shoe designed during the nineteenth century for playing croquet or tennis. By 1916 the United States Rubber Company introduced its own brand of rubber-soled canvas shoe called Keds and was followed in 1917 by the Converse Rubber Company with its All-Star shoe. Though other brands of tennis shoes appeared, the essential design did not change much until the 1960s, when a huge variety of tennis shoe designs appeared.

During the late 1960s many shoe designers began to experiment to improve athletic shoes. One of the most influential of these was a University of Oregon track coach named Bill Bowerman (1909–). Bowerman wanted to design a lightweight shoe with a traction sole especially for running. His improvements included providing shoes with a cushioned insole (a soft sole insert), replacing heavy canvas uppers (the portion of the shoe above the sole) with lighter nylon, and introducing the waffle outer sole, which he created by molding latex rubber with a kitchen waffle iron. Bowerman named his shoes and eventually named his company Nike, for the Greek goddess of victory.

Nike and other shoe manufacturers, such as Adidas and Spalding, made further developments to tennis shoes that not only made the shoes specialized for sports but made them more appealing as a fashion item. Thousands of amateur runners bought tennis

Though tennis shoes were developed for wear on European croquet lawns during the late 1800s, Americans adopted them for all-occasion use in the 1970s. *Reproduced by permission of © Royalty-Free/CORBIS.*

shoes during the jogging craze of the 1970s but soon began wearing tennis shoes for all occasions. Brightly colored nylon uppers and big, but lightweight, waffle soles became accepted as part of everyday wear. Fashion designers, such as Calvin Klein (1942–), began designing stylish tennis shoes. Soon the flashy tastes of the 1970s could be seen in tennis shoe designs; tennis shoes with sequins and satin uppers with high heels or platform soles were useless for sports but trendy on the disco dance floor.

The tennis shoe has remained an item of high fashion into the twenty-first century and is sold throughout the world. People in many countries across the globe wear tennis shoes for sports, as well as for comfortable everyday shoes. Many Europeans, however, do not wear sneakers as street shoes and consider the practice a vulgar American habit. Prices have risen dramatically since the first Keds tennis shoe was introduced in 1916, and many popular athletic shoes cost well over one hundred dollars. In spite of the high price tag, the shoes remain in high demand. The popularity of high-priced sneakers has even led to crime in rare instances, as some young people have been attacked and had their shoes stolen.

FOR MORE INFORMATION

Cheskin, Melvyn P. *The Complete Handbook of Athletic Footwear.* New York: Fairchild, 1987.

Kiefer, Michael. "Ode to the Sneaker: A Discourse on Laces, Lore and Sole With Soul." *Chicago* (May 1986): 164–68.

Vanderbilt, Tom. *The Sneaker Book.* New York: New York Press, 1998.

[*See also* **Volume 3, Nineteenth Century: Tennis Shoes**]

America Forges Ahead: 1980–2003

Historians have yet to come up with good labels for the 1980s and 1990s. The 1980s have been called the "Decade of Greed" because of the aggressive business growth of the time, and the 1990s have been labeled the "New Economy" or the "Internet Age," recognizing the extraordinary influence of high-tech industries. These labels focus attention on the economic changes of the time, yet they may not fully recognize the extent to which the United States dominated Western culture. In world politics, economic innovation, and popular culture, the United States was the single most dynamic and creative force in the world.

The new world order

At the beginning of the 1980s world politics were dominated by the Cold War (1945–91), a long-simmering conflict between the United States and the Soviet Union that forced nearly every country in the world to side with the capitalist, democratic United States or the Communist, state-run Soviet Union. Under American presidents Ronald Reagan (1911–) and George Bush (1924–), the United States began a program of weapon building like none in history. The Soviets struggled to keep up, but the American economy soon prevailed. By the late 1980s the Soviet system had begun to weaken and collapse, and by 1991 the entire Soviet Union collapsed

GAP

Gap is a successful worldwide chain of clothing stores, with many divisions, each of which sells variations of basic casual clothes. In 1969 Donald and Doris Fisher opened a small clothing and record store in San Francisco. Seven years later the company had grown enough to begin selling its stocks on the New York Stock Exchange, and the next year it opened a charitable foundation. In 1983 Millard Drexler became the company president. One of his first acts was to buy a small travel clothing store called Banana Republic, which became a profitable division of Gap, Incorporated, selling upscale "casual luxury" clothing. Over the next decades the company opened GapShoes, GapKids, and BabyGap. GapBody opened to sell underwear and sleepwear, and Old Navy, which opened in 1994 and is owned by Gap, sold discount casuals for the whole family.

Since the 1980s the Gap has become a multibillion-dollar business and a household word marketing such basics as T-shirts, blue jeans, and sweaters. Gap stores are designed to be accessible to busy shoppers who want to buy fashionable clothes cheaply. The stores are easy to recognize, as every Gap store has the same basic design and layout. The stores specialize in offering a few basic designs in a wide variety of trendy colors, and they receive whole new lines of clothing seven or eight times a year, making sure that the colors and styles stay up-to-date.

Beginning in 1987 Gap began to open the first of several hundred stores around the world. Not surprisingly, a Gap store in Paris, France, looks exactly like a Gap in New York or Hong Kong. Critics of the Gap disapprove of this mass production and marketing of fashion, claiming that it damages individuality with everyone buying the exact same clothes from the exact same store everywhere in the world. Others dislike the huge stores, which often change the tone and personality of the neighborhoods in which they are located. They say that because Gap is part of a large corporation it can sell clothes at lower prices, which drives smaller, locally owned stores out of business. Still others have called on Gap to take responsibility for the poor working conditions at the clothing factories in Mexico, Asia, and Central America where the company buys the clothes it sells. Regardless of the views on the chain, Gap continued to be a success into the twenty-first century.

This Gap store in San Francisco, California, looks the same as any other Gap store and sells much the same merchandise. *Reproduced by permission of AP/Wide World Photos.*

and broke into a number of smaller countries, many of which immediately embraced capitalism and democracy. Without a shot fired at the enemy, the United States had won its greatest victory.

With the Soviet Union gone, the United States was now the world's greatest superpower. With the world's biggest army and the world's strongest economy, U.S. power truly dominated the world. President George Bush, explaining the role that the United States would play in world politics in 1991, proclaimed the existence of a "new world order," with the United States promoting peace and prosperity as the world's policeman. One of its first actions in this role was waging the Gulf War against Iraq, a country that threatened to undermine stability in the Middle East. This short war lasted just a few weeks in 1991 but flared up again in 2003 when President George W. Bush (1946–) sent troops in to depose Iraqi leader Saddam Hussein (1937–). The United States's continued involvement in the Middle East created great hostility amongst Arabs who did not like Western society and helped fuel terrorist attacks such as the attacks on New York City's World Trade Center and the Pentagon on September 11, 2001. Though most Western countries supported the United States in the first war in Iraq, that support declined in the second war. Being the world's sole superpower was not easy for the United States.

Economic booms

Another area in which the United States led the world was economic growth. Fueled by the economic programs of President Reagan, who served from 1980 to 1988, the American economy boomed in the mid-1980s, as did the economies of most European countries and Japan, which had become a major economic competitor. Reagan cut taxes on the wealthiest people and gave businesses huge advantages. His economic programs created a climate where aggressive business practices were highly valued. American business expanded overseas, establishing factories in poor countries that could provide cheap labor and opening stores and branches in the more prosperous countries.

Though the economy declined between 1987 and 1992, a new surge under President William Jefferson Clinton (1946–) helped to sustain American economic supremacy. This new boom was driven by the growth of the computer industry, especially industry giant Microsoft, and the many offshoots of that industry, called the high-

POWER DRESSING

Power dressing, the wearing of expensive business clothing to indicate status, became fashionable among working men and women in the United States and Great Britain during the 1980s. At a time when jobs were plentiful and businesses were thriving, power dressing enabled people to convey an image of success. The centerpiece of a power dresser's wardrobe was a tailored business suit, or power suit. In addition, power dressing included expensive accessories: cellular phones, electronic date books, laptop computers, and luxury sports cars made by BMW, Jaguar, or Porsche. The goal of power dressing was to look like an executive whether you were or not.

For more than fifty years, the gray flannel suit had been a popular style for working men. But power suits were different. Power suits gave the wearer a look of authority and style that had previously been affordable to only the rich. Italian designer Giorgio Armani (1934–) created the most popular brand of power suit. Armani's custom suits were beyond the budgets of regular working men, but the demand for power suits encouraged Armani to introduce less expensive lines of ready-to-wear suits. These suits became a symbol of business success for fashionable white-collar working men.

Power dressing for women made even more of an impact. Before the 1970s most working women were confined to such traditional female occupations as secretaries, bookkeepers, and typists. By the 1980s, however, women were becoming lawyers, politicians, and corporate executives. To complement their new authority, women power-dressed. Such attire communicated the impression of confidence and authority. Power dressing enabled women to be taken seriously in a male-dominated corporate workplace.

Like men, women sought designer label clothing for their business wardrobe. Designers such as Karl Lagerfeld (1938–) and Valentino (1932–) offered fashionable business ensembles of jackets with large shoulder pads and straight skirts to be worn with color-coordinated shoes and handbags. Women softened their look by wearing blouses in muted colors under their suit jacket or blazer or accessorizing their outfit with an ornately designed scarf or pin.

Other than designers, power-dressing styles were influenced by celebrities and television shows. England's prime minister Margaret Thatcher (1925–) popularized tailored evening suits; Diana, princess of Wales (1961–1997), popularized hats, which usually were worn after work; and stars of nighttime soap operas of the 1980s such as *Dallas* (1978–91) and *Dynasty* (1981–89) popularized padded shoulders and costume jewelry.

tech industry or the "New Economy." Stock markets around the world soared and the economy was further boosted by the emergence of the Internet as a means of exchanging goods and information. Again, American businesses led the way. This boom finally ended around 2000, and a sustained recession, or economic downturn, was felt throughout the world in the first years of the twenty-first century.

Popular culture

Not only was the United States the dominant political and economic power in the 1980s and 1990s, it was also the world's leading producer of popular culture: movies, television, music, food, and more. The entertainers and movies that made a hit in the United States were soon exported throughout the West. Musicians such as Madonna (1958–) and Michael Jackson (1958–), and sports stars such as basketball player Michael Jordan (1963–), became world-wide celebrities. American filmmakers provided the majority of the world's films. American restaurants such as McDonald's and Burger King opened stores across the globe, including such once-forbidden spots as Russia and China.

The spread of popular culture meant that the world was becoming Americanized, and sometimes the world did not like it. In the countries of Europe, which had traditionally been the United States's greatest allies, or associates, hostility toward American dominance grew. French people protested the opening of a Disneyland amusement park in Paris, France, in the 1990s, and the European Economic Union worked hard to counter American economic dominance by easing trade between European countries and introducing a single currency to be used throughout Europe in the early twenty-first century. Hostility toward the United States was greatest in the Islamic countries of the Middle East and Far East. Facing these hostilities is perhaps the biggest challenge faced by the United States in its role as world leader.

Unlike the 1960s and 1970s, when politically oriented social groups and movements like the hippies, a group of young people who rejected conventional values and dress, and the Women's Liberation movement had a great effect on what people wore, clothing customs in the 1980s and beyond were rarely touched by world events. Fads were more highly influenced by the entertainment industry. While the consumption of high-priced and high fashion clothes increased in the 1980s, the general prosperity of people in Western countries meant that almost everyone had access to a range of comfortable and even stylish clothing and accessories.

FOR MORE INFORMATION

"About Gap Inc." *Gap Inc.* http://www.gapinc.com/about/about.htm (accessed on August 27, 2003).

Feinstein, Stephen. *The 1980s: From Ronald Reagan to MTV.* Berkeley Heights, NJ: Enslow Publishers, 2000.

Feinstein, Stephen. *The 1990s: From the Persian Gulf War to Y2K.* Berkeley Heights, NJ: Enslow Publishers, 2001.

Kallen, Stuart A. *The 1980s.* San Diego, CA: Lucent Books, 1999.

Kallen, Stuart A. *The 1990s.* San Diego, CA: Lucent Books, 1999.

Lomas, Clare. *20th Century Fashion: The 80s and 90s, Power Dressing to Sportswear.* Milwaukee, WI: Gareth Stevens, 2000.

Nevaer, Louis E. V. *Into—and Out of—the Gap: A Cautionary Account of an American Retailer.* Westport, CT: Quorum Books, 2001.

Clothing, 1980–2003

The years between 1980 and 2003 present all the complexities of modern costume. These decades saw a rise and fall in the status of high-profile clothing designers and their extravagant clothes; the sudden popularity of certain clothing items, often associated with youth-driven music trends; the impact of new technologies; the influence of celebrities on fashion; all set against a general trend to favor comfortable, casual clothes. These trends were a continuation of the trends that had characterized the second half of the twentieth century. But what made the period from the 1980s onward different was the speed with which styles changed and the amount of money directed toward clothing.

Working days, glamorous nights

After the 1970s, a decade in which the world of high fashion had fallen into disarray and people picked and chose amongst several acceptable styles, designer fashions came roaring back in the 1980s. High-profile European designers like Giorgio Armani (c. 1934–), Christian Lacroix (1951–), Karl Lagerfeld (1938–), Jean-Paul Gaultier (1952–), Azzedine Alaïa (c. 1940–), and others introduced daring, expensive lines of clothes to the praise of the fashion press. Wealthy people across Europe and in the United States flocked to Paris fashion shows and New York boutiques to purchase expensive originals, and lower-level designers and mass-market retail stores modeled their clothing lines on the more conservative efforts of the top names. This was the traditional way that fashions had been set, with designers leading the way in the creation of clothing styles.

New fashion designers were able to be bought, promoted, recreated because of one thing: money. During the early and mid-

1980s business exploded in the West and in the increasingly westernized Japan. Stock market traders, corporate executives, and even second-tier executives grew extremely wealthy in a climate where success in business was celebrated as the ultimate mark of achievement. These new cultural celebrities used clothes as one of the ways to demonstrate their wealth and power. American president Ronald Reagan (1911–) and his wife, Nancy (1923–), wore designer suits and gowns, and corporate leaders proudly extolled the merits of their favorite designers. For men the "power suit," a tailored suit, preferably by Giorgio Armani, was the symbol of success. Women dressed for power by day, with designer suits and business dresses, and for glamour by night, with extravagant gowns in the richest fabrics. These wealthy people were held up as cultural models and their clothing styles imitated on popular television shows like *Dynasty*

RALPH LAUREN AND CALVIN KLEIN

American designers Ralph Lauren (1939–) and Calvin Klein (1942–) both began their designing careers during the late 1960s, but it was in the 1980s that they became fashion superstars. At a time when designer fashion was identified with outlandish outfits modeled on Paris fashion runways, both Lauren and Klein created designer clothes for ordinary people.

Ralph Lauren

Lauren was born Ralph Lifschitz in Brooklyn, New York. Fascinated with fashion from an early age, he dropped out of college and apprenticed in the fashion industry by working at various clothing companies. In 1967 he got a job at Beau Brummel, designing the wide neckties in bright colors for which he would first become famous. By 1968 he launched his own line of men's clothes, which he called Polo. With the name Polo, Lauren said much about his design philosophy. The game of polo was associated with rich Europeans, and Lauren's designs came from classic European traditions. Often referred to as

"preppy English tweed" style, or "American country" style, Lauren's early designs, which included a variety of casual and semiformal wear, were updated versions of basic designs, sewn in classic materials, such as wool tweed and corduroy.

Besides his clothing, Lauren made other contributions to the fashion world. He licensed his designs (sold the right to manufacture them) to a range of clothing companies as long as the clothes bore his name, and he also branched out into many different areas of design. Following the success of his men's clothing line, Lauren introduced a line of women's clothes, followed by cosmetics, perfumes, bath towels, bed sheets, and even house paint, all with the unmistakable Lauren quality of traditional elegance. Though some have accused Lauren of being unoriginal and boring, many men and women find his designs to be comfortable and dependable. Other famous designers, such as Donna Karan (1948–) and Bill Blass (1922–2002), have praised Lauren for his contributions to classic style.

Calvin Klein

Calvin Klein was also born in Brooklyn. As a boy his interest in fashion led him to teach himself to

(1981–89) and *Dallas* (1978–91). The choices of the rich and their favored designers thus had a great impact on clothing.

The fashion boom of the 1980s was more international than ever before. Though Paris, New York, and London remained the true centers of world fashion, designers from Italy, especially the city of Milan, and from Japan also exerted a real influence on fashion. The Italians became associated with rich fabrics and classic cuts, while the Japanese are credited with boosting the popularity of the color black.

Not everyone could afford the clothing made by the big name European or Japanese designers, but in the 1980s there were real alternatives for those who still wanted to follow fashions. Top designers, such as Calvin Klein (1942–) and Ralph Lauren (1939–),

sew and sketch designs. He attended New York's High School of Art and Design and the Fashion Institute of Technology and, by 1968, he had established Calvin Klein Limited, his own line of clothing. Klein's designs were characterized by simple lines and subdued colors sewn in elegant, luxurious fabrics, like linen, silk, and cashmere.

Though Klein produced many different products, he is best known for his lines of underwear, blue jeans, and fragrances, such as Obsession and Eternity. One of Klein's major innovations in the fashion industry was his use of sexuality in advertising. Though many people were shocked and horrified by his use of sexual imagery, Klein became the first, and perhaps the most expert, at using sex to sell basic clothing like blue jeans at high prices.

During the socially conservative 1980s, Lauren and Klein helped create a major change in the way average people saw designer fashion. Where clothing designed by a high fashion designer was once seen as only for the wealthy, the styles created by Klein and Lauren were designed for everyday wear at the office or on a date. Their elegant styles succeeded simply because they made the average person feel like one of the elite.

Calvin Klein is best known for his jeans, fragrances, and provocative ads. *Reproduced by permission of Getty Images.*

offered high-end custom clothes, but they also offered a ready-to-wear line that had the high status of a designer name but at a more reasonable price. Many designers built international design empires, selling their brand-name clothes, perfumes, and accessories throughout the world.

Sex sells

One of the most important trends of the 1980s and 1990s was the emergence of open sexuality as an important element in clothing design. A variety of causes lead to the growing openness with which sexuality was displayed in this period. Perhaps the most important was the ongoing fitness boom that encouraged people of all ages, but especially young people, to pay a great deal of attention to getting their bodies in good shape. People wanted to show off their newly sculpted bodies and there were a variety of clothing options for those who wanted to flaunt it. Calvin Klein celebrated the human form with his underwear designs, which were made famous with an advertising campaign centered on towering billboards on the side of skyscrapers in New York City. Spandex, a high-tech, stretchy fabric, was used to create formfitting biking shorts and tights, and the Wonderbra, introduced in the mid-1990s, pushed women's breasts up and in to show off their cleavage. Designers created extremely clingy dresses, and supermodels, or high-profile models, and music celebrities such as Madonna (1958–), in the 1980s, and Ricky Martin (1974–), Britney Spears (1981–), and Christina Aguilera (1980–), in the 1990s, made a great public display of their sexuality. A youth trend in the 1990s for hip-hugging, low-riding pants and bare midriffs brought sexual display as far as the pre-teen market. By 2003 little was forbidden in the display of flesh.

The 1990s flight from fashion

The designer-worshipping fashion excesses of the 1980s crashed along with stock markets in 1987. Although designers still produced annual collections and fashion magazines highly praised them, the world retreated from its celebration of wealth and haute couture, or high fashion, in the late 1980s and early 1990s. With designers out of favor, the other dominant mode of determining clothing trends reemerged. As in the 1970s people took their clothing cues from popular music, from youth subcultures, from the more successful mass-market retailers, and from their own desire for comfort and personal expression. Once again designers began to take their cue from the streets.

Young people and their music were especially influential in the early 1990s. The grunge, or alternative rock, music scene that emerged out of Seattle, Washington, created a fashion trend favoring flannel shirts and ripped jeans, and it wasn't long before designers offered their own grunge collections. Hip-hop or rap music, which had once been the music of African Americans living in the inner city, went mainstream and brought with it a craze for extremely baggy jeans.

For the great majority of people, however, choices about clothing were dictated by the wearer's desire for casual comfort and by the minor variations in styles offered by major retailers. The trend toward casual business dress began in the 1980s with casual Fridays, when business dress codes were relaxed for the day, and became widespread among workers in the booming high-tech industries of the late 1990s. At work, men could wear chinos (a type of khaki pants) and a shirt without a tie, and women could wear more casual dresses and pants. For leisure time both men and women chose cotton pants and knit shirts, tennis shoes, sweatshirts, and other athletic clothes. The most popular outer wear was made of a fuzzy, high-tech fabric called polar fleece, which came in bright colors.

People had a huge range of choices about where to buy their clothes, from designer stores and department-store boutiques such as Ralph Lauren, Tommy Hilfiger, and Calvin Klein; to mid-range specialty retailers such as Gap and Old Navy; to mail order catalogs such as J. Crew, Lands' End, and L. L. Bean; to discount retailers like K-Mart, Wal-Mart, and Target. These stores offered clothes of reasonable quality with trendy styling.

RISE OF THE JAPANESE DESIGNER

Oriental designs had appealed to Western consumers since the beginning of trade between the two regions. But it was only in the 1960s that a Japanese-born designer, Kenzo Takada (1940–), first found success with his own designs in Paris, France. By the 1980s Japanese designers Rei Kawakubo (1942–), Issey Miyake (1938–), and Yohji Yamamoto (1943–) dazzled the West with their clothing. Their designs were futuristic and defied convention; their garments were often elaborately constructed, with odd panels, uneven hems and, in the famous words of Kawakubo, came in "black, black, black." Their clothes were quickly adopted by style-conscious Japanese youth and then found success among Europe's more daring trendsetters.

The Japanese trio enjoyed strong worldwide sales for their lines for many years. Their styles strongly influenced other fashion designers, as well as musicians and artists, but never achieved mainstream success. By 1984 many mass-market apparel makers were copying some of their unusual design elements, especially the oversized look, for the younger market. The largest impact the Japanese designers had on mainstream fashion was to make black the most popular color for clothing for much of the late 1980s and early 1990s.

Colors and details changed from season to season, but the basic garments remained the same.

FOR MORE INFORMATION

Carnegy, Vicky. *Fashions of a Decade: The 1980s.* New York: Facts on File, 1990.

Ewing, Elizabeth. *History of Twentieth Century Fashion.* Revised by Alice Mackrell. Lanham, MD: Barnes and Noble Books, 1992.

Feldman, Elane. *Fashions of a Decade: The 1990s.* New York: Facts on File, 1992.

Gaines, Steven S., and Sharon Churcher. *Obsession: The Lives and Times of Calvin Klein.* New York: Avon Books, 1995.

Gross, Michael. *Genuine Authentic: The Real Life of Ralph Lauren.* New York: Harper, 2003.

Lomas, Clare. *The 80s and 90s: Power Dressing to Sportswear.* Milwaukee, WI: Gareth Stevens, 2000.

Steele, Valerie. *Fifty Years of Fashion: New Look to Now.* New Haven, CT: Yale University Press, 1997.

Armani Suits

In the late 1970s and early 1980s, a suit fashioned by the celebrated and influential Italian designer Giorgio Armani (1934–) became the outfit of choice for wealthy, style-conscious males. Armani suits were known for their simple yet elegant design, their striking look, and their comfort. They were custom tailored and were meticulously cut to fit the form of the purchaser. A typical Armani suit generally featured three pieces: a fully-lined, three-button blazer with padded shoulders; a matching vest; and single-pleated trousers that were lined only in front, down to the knees. The suit was black, charcoal gray, or navy blue; it was soft or textured; and it was made of the highest quality wool, cotton, cashmere, silk, or linen.

During the 1980s the Armani suit projected authority and self-confidence and became the ultimate "power suit," a name given to suits that were meant to display the power, or at least the ambition, of the wearer. Armani suits were favored by Wall Street stockbrokers and Hollywood agents. They were regularly worn at the Academy Awards. The celebrities who favored them ranged from movie actor Richard Gere (1949–), who famously wore them on-screen in *American Gigolo* (1980), to basketball coach Pat Riley (1945–).

Armani's profile was so high that in 1982 he became the first fashion designer to appear on the cover of *Time* magazine

In the 1980s, an exquisitely tailored Armani power suit was a symbol of success. *Reproduced by permission of AP/Wide World Photos/Fashion Wire Daily.*

since Christian Dior (1905–1957) four decades earlier. Additionally, Armani employed his basic fashion philosophy, extravagant does not mean uncomfortable or overdone, in the simple, stylish suits he designed for women. His dark or neutral-colored jackets and pantsuits became standard attire for women in and out of the workplace.

FOR MORE INFORMATION

Celant, Germano, and Harold Koda, with Susan Cross and Karole Vail. *Giorgio Armani.* New York: Harry N. Abrams, 2000.

Giorgio Armani. http://www.giorgioarmani.com (accessed on August 27, 2003).

Baggy Jeans

Baggy pants on young men could be spotted early in the 1990s, but they remained a largely "underground" style, worn only by a limited number of people pushing the edge of style, until hip-hop replaced grunge as the dominant music form among urban teenagers. By the mid-1990s long baggy shorts became common. Youngsters now demanded that jeans, which had long been a major part of casual dress, be as baggy as possible, with waists several sizes too large revealing the upper band of underwear. Retailers like Gap and Old Navy introduced baggy lines of jeans. Designer Tommy Hilfiger (1951–) created an "urban prep" line, copying a street style he observed in which baggy denim was paired with crisp white button-up shirts.

Explanations vary as to why baggy jeans became so popular. Some claim that trendsetters in the hip-hop community adopted the style to copy the pants that prisoners are issued when they are incarcerated. Sagging pants, according to this theory, reflect the fact that prison inmates are not allowed to have belts, for fear they will hang themselves in their cells. Others contend that the fashion for baggy jeans originated with black basketball stars like Michael Jordan (1963–), who objected to the short shorts mandated for many years by the National Basketball Association and began to wear longer, baggier shorts. Still others believe that baggy jeans have their roots in the skateboarding and snowboarding communities, where participants needed freedom of movement but also wanted to look different from other people.

Whatever their origins, the baggy jeans trend had a profound effect on the sportswear industry. Jeans maker Levi's, which was slow to offer baggy jeans, saw its sales fall 15 percent from 1996 to 1998. While hip-hop fashions remained popular into 2003, signs emerged that the style was shifting back to formfitting and low-rise boot cut jeans, jeans that fit low on the waist and flare out at the ankle.

FOR MORE INFORMATION

George, Nelson. *Hip Hop America.* New York: Penguin, 1999.

Westbrook, Alonzo. *Hip Hoptionary: The Dictionary of Hip Hop Culture.* New York: Broadway Books, 2002.

[*See also* **Volume 3, Nineteenth Century: Blue Jeans**]

Casual Fridays

As computer software began to receive more and more media attention in the late 1980s, informal office situations and casual, even eccentric, clothes became identified with the wealth and creativity of the highly successful computer executives. Managers of other successful businesses began to wonder if this informal atmosphere could work to improve their own offices.

In 1991 Levi-Strauss, manufacturer of blue jeans and other casual wear, joined with the United Cerebral Palsy Association (UCPA) to launch a nationwide fund-raising event. "Casual Day," as it was called, would allow employees to buy the privilege of dressing more informally for the day by making a charitable contribution to UCPA. Many businesses joined in the project, and it was very successful, leading not only to more fund-raising casual days, but also to many businesses establishing a regular casual day, usually on Fridays.

Casual Fridays steadily increased in popularity. By 1996 a Levi-Strauss study found that 90 percent of American office workers were allowed to dress casually on Fridays, as opposed to 47 percent in 1993. Many business owners and managers found that allowing their employees one day of informality did increase their productivity and gave the office a more welcoming, relaxed atmosphere. Some noted that fewer workers were absent on Fridays than before the introduction of the casual day. Many banks expanded the policy, introducing casual summers. Some clothing manufacturers introduced new lines of clothing just for casual work dress.

Others did not approve of the new policy, however. In 1995 a group called Dress Right formed to ban casual Fridays, and some business magazines spoke out against the policy as bad business practice. In addition, the definition of casual was often open to debate, and this frequently led to endless office memos, forbidding items considered too casual, such as ragged blue jeans and halter tops. For the employee, choosing the appropriate clothes for casual days could be more difficult than dressing for a regular work day. For many men, whose regular office wear was a fairly simple dark suit and white shirt, casual Friday was the only work day where they were required to think about what to wear.

Casual Fridays originated in the often-informal United States, but in the late 1990s the idea was successfully exported to other countries as well. Office workers in Japan and Great Britain, for example, welcomed the occasional chance to dress more informally, and the new sales of casual business clothes gave a boost to some clothing manufacturers. By the late 1990s many businesses moved to an entirely "business casual" dress code.

FOR MORE INFORMATION

"Dressing Down: At the Firm, Casual Friday Is Anything But Relaxing." *Los Angeles Daily Journal* (May 14, 1999): 8.

Kemp, Kristen. "Casual Friday Clothing Fiascoes." *Cosmopolitan* (November 1999): 227.

Mannix, Margaret. "Casual Friday, Five Days a Week." *U.S. News and World Report* (August 4, 1997): 60.

Designer Jeans

Since their invention in the nineteenth century, the durable pants known as blue jeans or dungarees were commonly worn by cowboys and farmers and, later, children and teenagers. Starting in the late 1970s, however, a new kind of jean appeared in the marketplace. Called designer jeans, they were fashioned for style rather than practicality. They were worn skin-tight to accentuate the body's curves. Designer jeans were made with combinations of cotton, spandex, and Lycra, which allowed them to move and stretch with the body. Some were even made of suede and leather.

Traditional blue jeans were so named for an obvious reason: they were blue in color. But designer jeans came in all colors, starting with several shades of blue, black, gray, brown, olive, tan, and white. They also featured various fabric treatments, including bleached, with the color faded; acid-washed, or extremely bleached,

Model and actress Brooke Shields shows off her Calvin Klein designer jeans. *Reproduced by permission of AP/Wide World Photos.*

Calvin Klein Jeans

with streaks; and stone-washed, so as to look worn. Designer jeans also offered a variety of pant leg styles, from very snug to very loose. Some pants had zippers at their leg bottoms, and others were purposefully ripped.

Arguably the era's highest profile designer jeans featured the name of Gloria Vanderbilt (1924–), a celebrated American socialite and heiress of the Vanderbilt fortune. (The Vanderbilt family had been one of the wealthiest families in the United States, building their fortune in shipping and railroads in the late 1800s and early 1900s.) The Murjani Company worked with Vanderbilt to design and market Gloria Vanderbilt Jeans and sales of the sexy, super-tight-fitting jeans skyrocketed. They featured the Vanderbilt name on their back pocket and a trademark swan logo above the front pocket.

Other popular 1980s jeans brands were EJ Gitano, Jordache, Guess, Girbaud, Sergio Valente, Chic, Zena, and Sassoon. As the result of a TV ad featuring a bouncy lyric, "Ooh La La Sassoon," Sassoon jeans had special appeal for young girls. The ad conveyed the message that, if you really wanted to be part of the "in," or popular, crowd, you had better be wearing Sassoon jeans.

Designer jeans generally were more expensive than traditional jeans. Calvin Klein (1942–) won name recognition when he became the first designer to market the jeans at affordable prices. Their subsequent popularity may be attributed to the manner in which they were marketed by Klein. In a celebrated 1980 television ad, fifteen-year-old actress/model Brooke Shields (1965–) seductively declared, "Nothing comes between me and my Calvins." The commercial was controversial, and sales of Klein designer jeans soared.

While specific designer jean types went out of style in the late 1980s, the range of available blue jean styles remained endless.

FOR MORE INFORMATION

Finlayson, Iain. *Denim: An American Legend.* New York: Simon and Schuster, 1990.

Harris, Alice, and Bob Morris. *The Blue Jean.* New York: PowerHouse Books, 2002.

Rosenbloom, Jonathan. *Blue Jeans.* New York: Messner, 1976.

[*See also* **Volume 3, Nineteenth Century: Blue Jeans; Volume 5, 1980–2003: Baggy Jeans**]

Goth Style

The term goth, short for gothic, was used beginning in the 1980s to describe certain rebellious youths who had a very distinctive way of viewing the world, and an equally distinctive style of dress. The term gothic had been used since the sixteenth century to describe medieval northern European architecture and later to describe novels that had a shadowy, mysterious atmosphere. That dark atmosphere, as well as the fashions worn by the characters in gothic novels, became attractive to many young people who did not feel connected to the modern society in which they lived. These young people adopted the pale skin, dark hair, and dark clothes associated with gothic novels, as well as a gloomy, mystical outlook on life.

Modern goths, with their fondness for pale skin, dark hair, and black clothes, were inspired by the mysterious gothic novels of centuries past. *Reproduced by permission of © Jonathan Torgovnik/CORBIS.*

Goths borrowed some of the fashion styles from the punk rock subculture of the 1970s, including the punks' big black Doc Martens boots and shredded clothing. However, while the punks seemed ultramodern, the goths were drawn to a gentler, old-fashioned style. Along with ripped black stockings or T-shirts, a goth might wear a crushed purple velvet skirt or vest, old-style high button shoes, or black work boots worn with fishnet stockings. Most goths wore only black or very dark clothes, and many dyed their hair black as well. Goths of both sexes often wore dark eye makeup, black lipstick, and black nail polish. As with the punks, piercings and tattoos were common among goths, and many chose ancient Celtic designs, all in black.

Most goths thought of themselves as rebels, misfits, and outcasts and were proud that their style of dress was viewed as very strange by mainstream society. In the early twenty-first century, however, goth style began to make its appearance on fashion runways, at Hollywood parties, and at the mall. Designers like Marc Jacobs (1964–) included elements of goth style in his 2001 show, and actress Gwyneth Paltrow (c. 1973–) wore a black goth-style gown to the 2002 Academy Awards. Many young goths are proud of being outcasts and dislike what they call "weekend goths," who wear goth styles but do not live a goth lifestyle.

FOR MORE INFORMATION

Acker, Kerry. *Everything You Need to Know about the Goth Scene.* New York: Rosen Publishing Group, 2000.

Schoenberg, Nara. "Underground Goth Cult Rising to Surface." *Chicago Tribune* (January 13, 2003).

[*See also* **Volume 5, 1961–79: Punk sidebar on p. 946**]

Grunge

Grunge fashions, inspired by the look of popular Seattle-based rock bands like Nirvana and Pearl Jam, were a fashion sensation of the early to mid-1990s. The casual street look eventually became incorporated into the designs of high fashion.

The term grunge was originally a slang term for the heavy guitar-based brand of rock music distributed by the Seattle-based independent record label Sub Pop. Once the Sub Pop band Nirvana hit the top of the charts with its 1991 album *Nevermind,* grunge suddenly became the hottest music style in the United States. With the music revolution came a fashion upheaval as well. Grunge style, a working-class look highlighted by the flannel shirts, combat boots, and ripped jeans favored by suburban teenagers, was suddenly seen everywhere. Nirvana posed for the cover of *Rolling Stone* magazine, while lead singer Kurt Cobain (1967–1994) and another grunge heartthrob, Eddie Vedder (1965–) of the group Pearl Jam, both received pin-up treatment in teen magazines. In 1992 grunge fashions came to the big screen with the release of *Singles,* a feature film about a group of slackers, or unmotivated, lazy people, from Seattle, Washington. Featuring 1980s teen idol Matt Dillon as a long-haired, flannel-clad, wanna-be rock star, the movie was a box office hit and helped popularize the grunge look.

The high point of the grunge style may have been the "Grunge and Glory" photo spread in the December 1992 issue of *Vogue,* the

Grunge rockers Krist Novoselic, left, and Kurt Cobain of Nirvana set the trend with their flannel shirts and ripped jeans. *Reproduced by permission of © S.I.N./CORBIS.*

world's top fashion magazine. Designer Marc Jacobs (1964–) out-fitted his models in $500 to $1,400 designer flannel and corduroy ensembles, supposedly representing a new style fresh from the thrift stores of Seattle. Jacobs followed that up with his Spring-Summer 1993 women's collection featuring over-sized flannel shirts, slouchy sweaters, and chunky army boots paired with floral print, vintage-looking dresses. The fashion line proved to be a commercial disaster, but few can deny its impact. For the next few years flannel shirts and other grunge staples could be seen on the racks at such mass-market shops as K-Mart and J. C. Penney.

FOR MORE INFORMATION

Azerrad, Michael. *Come As You Are: The Story of Nirvana.* New York: Doubleday, 1994.

Clancy, Deirdre. *Costume Since 1945.* New York: Drama Publishers, 1996.

True, Everett. *Live Through This: American Rock in the Nineties.* London, England: Virgin, 2001.

Polar Fleece

Zip-front jackets, vests, and other clothing items made from polar fleece, a trademarked synthetic, or man-made, fabric with a soft pile, emerged as tremendously popular cold-weather apparel for men, women, and children in the late 1990s and into the twenty-first century. The fad for polar fleece and related fabrics reflected widespread interest in outdoor adventure sports and the rugged lifestyle.

Polar fleece was the product of a Massachusetts textile company called Malden Mills that had enjoyed some success with fake-fur products over the years. Around 1979 the company began devoting resources to creating a lightweight synthetic fabric similar to a baby blanket it made. It began a partnership with Patagonia, a California-based maker of outdoor gear for hiking enthusiasts. The result was a fabric originally called bunting, which managed to retain body heat, keep moisture away from the skin, and still be lightweight and durable. Patagonia's first pile jacket, made from the

Malden Mills bunting, was its first big selling item for the hiking-gear company in the early 1980s.

Over the next decade outdoor-sports enthusiasts rose in number, taking up white-water rafting and mountain climbing in large numbers, and the outdoor apparel market blossomed to an estimated five billion dollars by the late 1990s. Fleece pullovers and other items soon emerged as a mass-market trend, advertised by companies like Old Navy. Even American designers like Donna Karan (1948–) and Tommy Hilfiger (1951–) began using polar fleece and its knockoffs in a range of items. Many of the garments seemed unisex and to denote the wearer as an outdoor-sports enthusiast. An increase in books recounting extreme-adventure exploits in the late 1990s captured the public fascination at the time, as did a marked trend toward adopting another symbol of the rugged outdoorsy life: the sport-utility vehicle.

Developed to keep outdoor-sports enthusiasts warm, polar fleece became a mass-market trend.
Reproduced by permission of © Rick Gomez/CORBIS.

FOR MORE INFORMATION

Espen, Hal. "Fleeced." *New York Times* (February 15, 1998).

Forstenzer, Martin. "On and Off the Beaten Path: Outdoor Gear Isn't Just for the Adventurous Anymore." *New York Times* (May 16, 1998).

Mott, Patrick. "With Enough Versatility to Put Polyester to Shame, Polartec Has Become the Synthetic King of the Textile Industry." *Los Angeles Times* (January 28, 1997): 5.

Spandex

Spandex, also known as Lycra, is a synthetic, or man-made, stretch fabric that gained immense popularity in the 1980s in a range of clothing items, beginning with biking shorts. Its formfitting properties quickly caught on with a younger, body-conscious crowd, and by the 1990s the apparel industry was using spandex and spandex blends in tights, bodysuits, T-shirts, pants, skirts, and even men's shirts. Spandex leggings, usually in black and worn with a baggy sweatshirt that covered the hips, were a popular casual style for young women throughout the 1990s.

Spandex is often known by its trade name, Lycra, which was introduced by American chemical company DuPont in 1959. Technically, Lycra is a fiber that DuPont researchers developed as an alternative to the latex-based rubber used in women's girdles and bras of that era. Lycra was a vast improvement over latex, for it could stretch to six hundred times its original length but return to its original shape, unlike rubber, which could overstretch. It was used in support pantyhose in the 1960s and then in swimwear later that decade. The French Olympic ski team wore Lycra garments for the 1968 Winter Olympic Games, and soon athletic-gear makers began using it. It proved especially popular in mid-thigh-length shorts worn by bicycle racers. By the 1980s, as the fitness trend reached a peak in the West, trendsetters began wearing the shorts on the street. French designer Azzedine Alaïa (c. 1940–) and his revolutionary formfitting dresses, which often used Lycra blends, gained a following among fashion models in the mid-1980s. In 1985 American designer Donna Karan (1948–) launched her first collection, which included Lycra-constructed bodysuits and skirts that were proclaimed as the first major innovation in some years.

Spandex proved such a popular fabric in the garment industry that by 1987 DuPont had trouble meeting worldwide demand. In the 1990s a variety of other items made with Spandex proved popular, including a successful line of body-shaping foundation garments sold under the trade name Bodyslimmers. As the decade progressed shirts, pants, dresses, and even shoes were being made with spandex blends, and mass-market retailers like Banana Republic were using it for menswear.

Originally used in women's undergarments and swimwear, spandex came to be a principal fabric for athletic-gear makers. *Reproduced by permission of © Royalty-Free/CORBIS.*

FOR MORE INFORMATION

Carnegy, Vicky. *Fashions of a Decade: The 1980s.* New York: Facts on File, 1990.

Dullea, Georgia. "The Lean Look on the Beach." *New York Times* (July 6, 1988): C8.

Hamilton, William L. "Lycra's New Reach: Et Tu, J. Crew?" *New York Times* (August 27, 2000).

"Spandex." *Newsweek* (Winter 1997): 24A.

Sweatshirts

Soft, long-sleeved pullover garments usually made of a cotton or cotton/polyester blend knit fabric that is soft and fleecy on the inside, sweatshirts have long been worn by athletes while warming up, watching from the sidelines, or cooling off after exercising. They began to be worn by nonathletes as well during the 1960s and were actually adopted by designers as part of their collections in the 1980s. By the 2000s sweatshirts were one of the most common parts of a typical person's everyday wardrobe and came in many different fabrics and styles.

The word sweatshirt was first used during the mid-1920s to describe the simple pullover jerseys, usually gray, that athletes wore before and after workouts. During the 1930s Abe and Bill Feinbloom, who owned the Knickerbocker Knitting

Worn by athletes in the 1920s, sweatshirts got the designer treatment in the 1980s. At the turn of the twenty-first century, sweatshirts were a part of almost everyone's wardrobe. *Reproduced by permission of © Jeff Curtes/CORBIS.*

Company, came up with a technique for applying letters to the knitted sweatshirts. They also designed a sideline sweatshirt, with a hood and a zipper, intended for football players to wear while sitting out of the game. Their company eventually became Champion, one of the best-known American manufacturers of athletic wear.

Sweatshirts were still worn mainly by athletes until the 1960s, when sweatshirts displaying the names of colleges and universities became popular with students. The trend toward informal fashion during the 1960s brought sweatshirts out of the locker rooms and onto the streets, as young people began to dress for comfort instead of following formal dress codes.

It was in the 1980s, however, that sweatshirts went from casual wear to high fashion. During the 1980s fitness fads like jogging and aerobics became very popular. The layered look was also fashionable during the 1980s, and sweatshirts layered well over T-shirts and jeans or spandex leggings. The popular 1983 movie *Flashdance* even started a craze for ripped sweatshirts such as those worn by the movie's star, Jennifer Beals (1963–). Many people did not want to wear just any sweatshirt; in the image conscious 1980s they demanded sweatshirts with a designer brand name. Upscale designers and retailers filled that need. An extreme example of the designer sweatshirt was a silk sweatshirt, designed by French designer Hermes, which sold for $650. American designer Norma Kamali (1945–) spread the sweatshirt's appeal even further when she designed a range of women's fashions made out of soft, fleecy sweatshirt material. Loose and comfortable, sweatshirts became a basic part of almost everyone's wardrobe, and their popularity continued into the twenty-first century.

FOR MORE INFORMATION

Carnegy, Vicky. *Fashions of a Decade: The 1980s.* New York: Facts on File, 1990.

Feldman, Elane. *Fashions of a Decade: The 1990s.* New York: Facts on File, 1992.

Wonderbra

The Wonderbra is a push-up bra that plunges at the front center, pulling the breasts together to create an elevated cleavage line. Based on the concept of the padded brassiere, the Wonderbra was introduced in the United States in 1994 and was quickly imitated by numerous competitors. The bra encouraged the trend in the United States in the late 1990s and early 2000s favoring high, pushed-up breasts.

The first padded brassieres were introduced in the 1960s, at a time when full-breasted women like actresses Jane Russell (1921–), Jayne Mansfield (1933–1967), and Marilyn Monroe (1926–1962) were considered the sexual ideal. Females who were not fully endowed in the bust area began stuffing their brassieres with facial tissues to enhance the look of the breast size. Recognizing a possible market for those women who wanted to look bustier than their natural figure allowed, lingerie manufacturers began designing lines of bras with cups that were padded with synthetic, or man-made, fibers. Since the 1960s padded bras have been so popular that one style or another has remained on the market.

The Wonderbra was created by Canadian designer Louise Poirier in 1964. With fifty-four separate elements, the bra was designed to dramatically alter the shape and direction of cleavage. The bra was not marketed for nearly thirty years. In 1994, after becoming a huge hit in Great Britain, the Wonderbra was introduced in the United States by the Bali Company, a division of the Sara Lee Corporation. The bras became an immediate sensation, drawing much media attention for the dramatic reshaping they gave to even small-breasted women.

Wonderbras are designed in three shapes, referred to as "degrees," so that women may choose the desired degree of enhancement. The first degree is found in lift bras that are lightly lined. The second degree appears in the padded and add-a-size models. The third degree, the design with the most dynamic shape enhancement, comes in the form of push-up bras. Push-up bras feature puffy padding known as "cookies." On some models the cookies are actually removable.

In 2001 Wonderbra introduced the Air Wonder model for "high altitude cleavage." With this futuristic model, a woman can pump up her bra cups to the size she chooses. A mini pump is included in each package.

FOR MORE INFORMATION

Fontanel, Beatrice. *Support and Seduction: A History of Corsets and Bras.* New York: Harry N. Abrams, 1997.

"Our Heritage: How It All Began–Wonderbra." *Sara Lee Intimate Apparel.* http://www.balinet.com/history_wonderbra.html (accessed on August 27, 2003).

[*See also* **Volume 4, 1900–18: Brassiere**]

Headwear, 1980–2003

The early 1980s brought a return of interest in high fashion after the comfort trend of the 1970s, which saw many people rejecting designer clothing. Fashion designers became celebrities by marketing collections of ready-to-wear (off-the-rack) clothing, cosmetics, and accessories to the huge middle class. Hairstylists became similarly celebrated, creating looks for film stars and television actors and then marketing hair care products for the general public. The wealthy also continued to influence fashion. One of the most celebrated trendsetters for hair and clothing was Lady Diana, princess of Wales (1961–1997).

With the formality of business attire so popular at the beginning of the 1980s, hairstyles were more rigid. Women wore stiff, perfectly styled hair. Either short or long, these styles were noted for their careful styling and the liberal amounts of gels and sprays that held them in place. Men adopted hairstyles that were meant to look casual and carefree but actually took a lot of work. The stars of the popular television show *Miami Vice* (1984–89), Don Johnson and Philip Michael Thomas wore the latest hairstyles for men, including the carefully maintained shadow of stubble on Johnson's chin.

By the 1990s hairstyles became more casual and more differentiated. Both men and women embraced individuality. In general, people abandoned the stiff styles of the 1980s and wore more natural, loose hairstyles. Women's styles, whether long or short, were worn loose and straight. Men, for the most part, kept their hair clipped short and their faces clean-shaven.

Hair coloring, for both men and women, was a popular and accepted way to change or enhance a particular hairstyle. However, wigs had dropped from fashion. Those with thinning hair relied more frequently on hair-growth stimulants such as Rogaine.

FOR MORE INFORMATION

Carnegy, Vicky. *Fashions of a Decade: The 1980s.* New York: Facts on File, 1990.

Cosgrave, Bronwyn. *The Complete History of Costume and Fashion: From Ancient Egypt to the Present Day.* New York: Checkmark Books, 2000.

Feldman, Elane. *Fashions of a Decade: The 1990s.* New York: Facts on File, 1992.

Mullet

Man with a mullet. Fans of the hairstyle, which was short on the top and sides and long in the back, included musicians and other celebrities as well as common people. *Reproduced by permission of © Ken Settle.*

Mullet is one of many names given to hair that is cut short on the top and sides and grown long in the back. The name mullet can be traced to the 1967 film *Cool Hand Luke* in which a prison inmate called men from the U.S. South who wore long hair "mulletheads," after a popular southern fish called mullet.

During the 1980s fashions reflected the influence of the punks, who wore their hair raggedly cut to different lengths and shaped into spikes. At the same time gays and lesbians began to challenge society's ideas of gender identity. They created androgynous styles that could be worn by either men or women. By cutting their hair short on top and wearing it long in back, they combined the uneven cuts of the Punks with a look that combined the masculine and the feminine. Many rock musicians of the late 1980s wore the mullet, including glam rock stars David Bowie (1947–) and Lou Reed (1942–). Up-and-coming female musicians Joan Jett (1960–) and Pat Benatar (1952–) wore crisply cut mullets to give themselves a strong, hard-edged look, while pop singer Michael Bolton (1953–) wore a flowing mullet that suggested a romantic masculinity.

By the mid-1990s the mullet began to be denounced by fashion commentators as a terrible fashion mistake. Some mullet nicknames are descriptive: 10/90 (refers to the ratio of hair on top to hair in the back), sholo (short-long), and business-in-front-party-out-back. Others identify the style with the American South where the mullet seemed extremely prevalent: Tennessee Top Hat and Kentucky Waterfall. Country music singer Billy Ray Cyrus (c. 1961–) wore a mullet and his hit song of the late 1990s, "Achy Breaky Heart," gave rise to another of the mullet's many nicknames: "Achy Breaky Mistakey." Jokes about the mullet have become widespread, with hundreds of Internet Web sites devoted to mullet humor. Nevertheless, the mullet continues to be a hairstyle worn by some people.

FOR MORE INFORMATION

Larson, Mark, and Barney Hoskyns. *The Mullet: Hairstyle of the Gods.* New York: Bloomsbury Publishing, 2000.

Jennifer Aniston's long and layered "Rachel" haircut was widely copied in the United States and Great Britain. *Reproduced by permission of NBC Television/Courtesy of Getty Images.*

Rachel Haircut

Television actress Jennifer Aniston (1969–) sparked a worldwide style craze in 1995 when her distinctive shag hairstyle was copied by women everywhere. Dubbed the "Rachel," after the name of her character, Rachel Green, on NBC's long-running hit sitcom *Friends,* the popular hairstyle helped Aniston emerge as the breakout star of the show's ensemble cast.

Friends debuted in 1994, steadily building a large and faithful audience, particularly among young, college-educated women. During its first season on the air, Aniston's charming coffee bar waitress Rachel Green was but one of six leads contending for the attention of viewers. Style trendsetters began to take notice in the second season, however, when Aniston unveiled a new hairstyle. A fresh variation on the shag haircut invented by New York salon legend John Sahag a generation earlier, Aniston's Rachel hairstyle fell just a bit below the shoulder and featured long layers all over. It was created especially for her by stylist Chris McMillan of Los Angeles' Estilo salon, who also created the stylish cuts for the show's other female casts members. McMillan later revealed that inspiration for the Rachel came about by accident as he worked to grow out Aniston's bangs over a series of cuts. The stylist then employed Velcro rollers to give her hair a full look.

The Rachel soon became the must-have hairdo among stylish women across the United States and also in Great Britain, where *Friends* was immensely popular. Not since Farrah Fawcett's blonde wings of the 1970s had the public reacted with such fervor to a hairstyle. Aniston eventually grew out the look and returned to a less trendsetting hairstyle but variations of the Rachel haircut were still popular in 2003.

FOR MORE INFORMATION

Bonner, Mike. *Jennifer Aniston.* Philadelphia, PA: Chelsea House, 2002.

Mendez, Teresa. "Off the Small Screen and into the Closet." *Christian Science Monitor* (March 26, 2003).

Rogaine

Rogaine is the brand name for a drug called minoxidil, developed, manufactured, and marketed by the Upjohn Pharmaceuticals Company. First offered to the public in 1988, minoxidil was promoted as the first successful cure for baldness. With an estimated 66 percent of men experiencing some hair loss by the age of thirty-five, according to Upjohn, and many women who also have hair loss, the new drug had many potential users hoping for a miracle cure. Within a few years, however, it became apparent that its effects were real, but short of miraculous.

Throughout the ages men have sought cures for baldness, mostly without success. Upjohn discovered the effects of minoxidil by accident in the mid-1970s. Researchers noticed that the subjects in a study concerning high blood pressure began to grow hair on their heads and faces. Soon they dropped the blood pressure tests and began to test the new drug as a cure for baldness. Once tests were complete, they introduced the new drug to the public in the form of a lotion named Rogaine, available by doctor's prescription.

Upjohn counted on men's desperation to find a cure for baldness to sell their product. They also introduced the first advertisements for a prescription drug that directly addressed the public. Their television and print ads for Rogaine discussed a problem that many men, and some women, had been afraid to talk about. People rushed to try the new product. By 1991, just three years after its introduction, over two million men worldwide used Rogaine, and by 1992 worldwide sales had reached $200 million.

The new drug was not without problems, however. Rogaine only successfully grew hair on about 10 percent of those who used it. Another 35 percent grew soft, short fuzz rather than normal hair. For many the drug did not work at all. In addition, it was fairly expensive to use, about seven hundred dollars for the first year and three hundred to six hundred dollars each year after that. The reality of the drug's performance hurt sales, but in 1995 Upjohn got permission from the Food and Drug Administration to sell the product over-the-counter, without a prescription, and many more people tried the drug, which was still used as a lotion. The company has made other efforts to improve sales, marketing a special Rogaine for women and offering a money-back guarantee.

FOR MORE INFORMATION

Beach, Pat. "Spraying for Deliverance." *GQ–Gentlemen's Quarterly* (January 1998): 80.

Webster, Donovan. "Re-Seeding Hairlines." *Men's Health* (February 1997).

Welcome to Rogaine.com. http://www.rogaine.com (accessed on August 27, 2003).

Body Decorations, 1980–2003

Since the 1980s body decoration and accessories have become a highly lucrative business. The intense interest in designer fashions in the 1980s created a demand for cosmetics, jewelry, handbags, and other items made by these makers of high fashion. For many, these accessories, with their designer labels or distinctive scents, were the only way to afford designer luxuries. At the beginning of this period the brand names of a few designers, such as Gucci and Prada, were the most sought after, but by the twenty-first century a multitude of brands offered men and women accessories in a variety of styles. Some social groups began to identify themselves by the brand names they wore rather than the particular style of accessory they chose. Some wore Tommy Hilfiger's (1951–) fashion lines, while others preferred Calvin Klein's (1942–) selections, for example.

As brand names rose in popularity, some people sought out unique adornments to set themselves apart. During the 1990s and into the twenty-first century, body piercing and tattooing became increasingly popular, especially among youth. The unique designs permanently drawn on the skin and the collection of jewelry pierced into the body were once only worn by groups such as punks. But by the 1990s these adornments had become accepted by a wider group of people, and many high school and college students chose to tattoo themselves and pierce their belly buttons, noses, or tongues.

Beginning in the 1980s the most coveted perfumes, colognes, lotions, and makeup were only available at high-end retail stores, but by the late 1990s people seeking more convenience had started buying their cosmetics through the mail, over the Internet, and in grocery stores. These changes did not reflect an abandonment of brand name status, as these outlets started to carry luxurious products.

FOR MORE INFORMATION

Gay, Kathlyn. *Body Marks: Tattooing, Piercing, and Scarification.* Brookfield, CT: Millbrook Press, 2002.

Graves, Bonnie B. *Tattooing and Body Piercing.* Mankato, MN: LifeMatters, 2000.

Steele, Valerie. *Fifty Years of Fashion: New Look to Now.* New Haven, CT: Yale University Press, 1997.

Backpack Purses

A woman carrying a small dog in a backpack purse. The backpack purse gained popularity in the 1990s for its stylishness as well as its practical qualities. *Reproduced by permission of © Pat Doyle/CORBIS.*

For a time in the mid-1990s legions of women began carrying their necessities in small, stylish backpacks instead of purses. The accessory proved to be a popular and practical alternative to the handbag.

The origin of the backpack as a fashion item is traced to Italian designer Miuccia Prada (c. 1949–), who had inherited her family's successful Milan luggage firm, Fratelli Prada. With her new husband, purse manufacturer Patrizio Bertelli (1946–), Prada began introducing stylish new items, including a practical little backpack made from the nylon material that her grandfather's company had long used to cover its newly made steamer trunks, large box-like suitcases used for travel by ship in the nineteenth and early twentieth centuries. The backpacks, with a small, triangular silver "Prada" logo attached, began selling in department stores in the early 1980s, though the company was virtually unknown in the North American market at the time. A ready-to-wear line was launched in 1989, and Miuccia Prada's elegant designs soon caught on with young, fashion-conscious women. The Prada backpack became a highly coveted status symbol around 1994, and part of its appeal was the hard-to-spot little silver triangle. They retailed for about four hundred dollars, and the company quickly launched a line of them in a multitude of sizes, colors, and fabrics. From there knockoffs, or reproductions, of the Prada item quickly caught on with mobile urban women, and by 1995 countless variations in leather, vinyl, and an array of other fabrics and colors were accounting for about 60 percent of the purse market in some retail sectors. Considered more practical than a purse, as well as safer on city streets, the backpack gained popularity for its practical qualities as well as its stylishness.

FOR MORE INFORMATION

Hessen, Wendy. "Backpacks: The New Basic." *WWD* (January 3, 1995): S14.

Meadus, Amanda, and Wendy Hessen. "Backpacks Fuel Mass Market." *WWD* (September 12, 1994): 6.

Rotenier, Nancy. "Antistatus Backpacks, $450 a Copy." *Forbes* (June 19, 1995): 118.

Gucci Bags

In 1921 Guccio Gucci (1881–1953) opened a small store in Florence, Italy, where he sold luggage and saddlery, accessories for horseback riders. Over the decades Gucci's business grew into an internationally renowned company that manufactured and distributed stylish, handsomely crafted personal items, including watches, shoes, ties, jewelry, suitcases, and scarves. Among the most popular and coveted Gucci products were handbags: a bag that is designed for women and normally used for carrying money, perfume, makeup, and other small items.

The trademark Gucci handbag, which featured a bamboo handle, was first produced in 1947. In the late 1960s, fashion trendsetter Jacqueline Kennedy Onassis (1929–1994), former U.S. first lady, helped popularize a Gucci handbag that featured a long strap, allowing it to be carried over the shoulder. These bags came to be known as the "Jackie O," with the "O" standing for "Onassis," the name she took upon marrying Greek shipping tycoon Aristotle

MILAN FASHION SCENE

A northern, industrial Italian city with little of the allure of Rome or Florence, Italy, Milan was home to a number of ambitious textile producers and clothing designers. In the late 1970s they began staging fashion shows in Milan to promote Italian designers. Representatives from upscale American department stores began flocking to the city to place large orders from the collections of up-and-coming new talents like Giorgio Armani (c. 1934–), Laura Biagiotti (1943–), Gianfranco Ferre (1944–), and Gianni Versace (1946–1997). Foreign journalists admired the new Italian styles as well.

Milan's runways presented a new style that caught on everywhere: though its shows were sometimes a bit theatrical and over-the-top, the models exuded a modern, athletic silhouette, or shape, that fit in perfectly with the era. The clothes, however, were the real appeal: they were simple, sexy, well made from an array of luxurious fabrics, and sold well. Within ten years of launching his company in 1975 with a man-tailored suit that became a must-have for an entire generation of fashionable women, Armani proved Milan's biggest success. For many years Armani's main rival was Ferre, and later Versace. Other top names in the Milan scene were Biagiotti, the Krizia label, and Missoni; the Fendi family of Rome even began staging their runway shows in Milan.

In the 1980s the Milan shows grew more extravagant and Armani was often hailed as the

Italian designer Gianni Versace, left, was one of the best designers on the Milan fashion scene. *Reproduced by permission of AP/Wide World Photos.*

king of Milan. In the 1990s new names joined the roster of shows held at two hotels near one another, the Principe and the Palace, including Dolce and Gabbana, Prada—a venerable luggage firm reshaped by the founder's design-conscious heir, Miuccia Prada—and the once-scorned house of Gucci, revitalized by American designer Tom Ford.

Onassis (c. 1900–1975) after the assassination of her first husband, President John F. Kennedy (1917–1963). By the 1980s brand name products had become especially popular and Gucci bags were among the most coveted handbags on the market.

Gucci handbags come in a range of sizes and styles. They are small or medium-sized, made of leather, canvas, and suede, and feature zippered compartments and metal locks or magnetic snap closures. Some have adjustable straps, usually made of leather. Gucci bags may be black with tan leather trim, blue and white with a leaf-and-flower design, or tan and brown with light caramel-colored trim. Many Gucci handbags feature a red and green stripe down their center and a metal Gucci logo. Some are so small that they are more like purses, small bags, or pouches primarily used for carrying money.

Gucci handbags, like all Gucci products, are prized by consumers as symbols of status. For this reason the commercial marketplace regularly is flooded with counterfeit Gucci items. Genuine Gucci bags are high priced, retailing in the many hundreds, and even thousands, of dollars and featuring serial numbers to confirm their authenticity.

FOR MORE INFORMATION

Anderson, Susan Heller. "Milan Comes of Age as a Fashion Capital." *New York Times* (October 13, 1977): C1, C12.

Goldstein, Lauren. "Milan Versus Paris: Fashion's Great Debate Isn't about Skirt Length or Heel Height, but Which Capital Makes the Trends." *Time International* (March 24, 2003): 66.

Johnson, Anna. *Handbags: The Power of the Purse.* New York: Workman Publishing, 2002.

Leg Warmers

During the 1970s a fitness craze swept the United States. Jogging and fast movement exercise classes called aerobics became popular leisure activities. Fashion followed the exercise trend, and it soon became fashionable to dress like an athlete, whether or not one actually participated in fitness activities. Specialty shoes, sweat clothes, leotards, and tights became fashionable for street wear, and over these it was popular for women to layer knitted leg warmers, tubes of fabric worn on the leg, reaching from knee or thigh to ankle.

Often made of wool or cotton and knitted like a big, loose, footless sock, leg warmers were commonly used by dancers to keep their leg muscles warm and flexible while wearing dance tights and

Model Christie Brinkley wearing a pink leotard and hot pink leg warmers. The 1970s fitness craze led to the 1980s leg warmers craze. *Reproduced by permission of © Bettmann/CORBIS.*

leotards. Actress Jane Fonda (1937–), who began a new career as a fitness teacher during the 1980s, encouraged those who bought her books and watched her videos to dress like dancers, in leotards, tights, and leg warmers, in order to feel more like athletes themselves. Along with Fonda, popular films, such as *Flashdance* (1983) and *Footloose* (1984), helped to popularize leg warmers.

Leg warmers went out of style by the late 1980s, but they returned in the early twenty-first century. Inspired by Japanese cartoons popular in the West, these modern leg warmers were likely to be made of cotton, leather, fleece, nylon, or faux fur and flared out below the knee.

FOR MORE INFORMATION

Bailey, Bill, and Frank Hoffman. *Arts and Entertainment Fads.* New York: Haworth, 1990.

Sewall, Gilbert T., ed. *The Eighties: A Reader.* Reading, MA: Addison-Wesley, 1997.

Sunless Tanning Lotion

During the 1920s a tanned complexion became associated with youth and vigor as more and more people began pursuing active lifestyles. Tanned skin remained in style for several decades. In the 1960s several sunless tanning lotions, which imitate the tanning effect of the sun by darkening the skin with chemical reactions, were marketed for those too busy indoors to get a suntan and for those with fair complexions who did not tan easily. Within a few hours of applying sunless tanning lotion, the skin would change color. However, early products produced an unnatural orange color that was often streaky and uneven.

During the mid-1980s it began to become important to people to stay out of the sun. Scientists had begun to publicize the damaging effects of constant excessive sun exposure. Partially due to changes in the earth's atmosphere caused by pollution, skin cancer had become one of the most common types of cancer. Experts warned that sunbathing was unhealthy and recommended wearing clothes, hats, and strong sunscreens when out in the sun.

However, tanned skin still remained in fashion. Manufacturers responded to people's health concerns about tanning in the sun by developing and improving their sunless tanning products. By the end of the 1980s almost every major suncare and cosmetics manufacturer had produced a sunless tanning lotion. Sunless tanning remained popular, and by 2003 a sunless tanning pill was in development, which promised to chemically reproduce the look of a suntan.

FOR MORE INFORMATION

Foltz-Gray, Dorothy. "A Tan for All Seasons: A Cautious Paleface Screens the New Crop of Sunless Tanners." *Health* (September 1995).

[*See also* **Volume 5, 1961–79: Tanning**]

Tattooing

Tattooing is the art of decorating the body with permanent pictures or symbols by pushing ink under the skin with sharp implements. Tattoos have been used by many different cultures, and in each culture the tattooed art has its own meaning. The English word tattoo comes from the Polynesian word *tatao,* meaning "to tap," which describes the technique by which sharp spines filled with color were tapped into the skin to make tribal designs. People in the 1980s wore tattoos of specific symbols to identify themselves as part of a particular social group. Their tattoos set them apart from mainstream society but were also visible signs by which they could recognize each other.

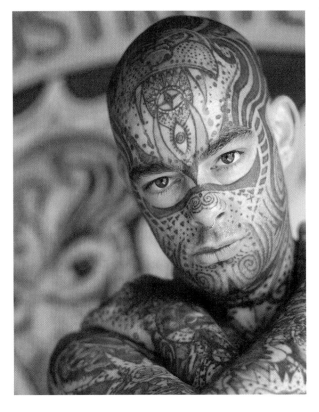

A man covered with intricate and colorful tattoos. *Reproduced by permission of Photo Researchers, Inc.*

Tattooing is an ancient and widespread practice. Tattoos have been found on the bodies of mummies thousands of years old, and certain tribes, such as Polynesians and the Maori of New Zealand, have used tattoos for centuries as a mark of membership in the tribe and a symbol of strength earned through pain. Modern tattooing began in 1900 when an American named Samuel O'Reilly invented the first electric tattoo machine. Most tattoo artists and their customers were outside the mainstream of society. However, many people who would never have dreamed of wearing a tattoo were fascinated with the art, and they lined up at carnivals and sideshows to gawk at elaborately tattooed men or women. Throughout most of the nineteenth and twentieth centuries, tattoos were considered low class and vulgar among Americans and Europeans, a common adornment for criminals and drunken sailors.

By the 1970s and 1980s tattoos had become part of fashion trends developed by small groups seeking to create distinctive looks to identify with their peers. Beginning in the 1970s many youth adopted a punk style, wearing outlandish clothing and hairstyles to announce the separation they felt from mainstream society. Much of the intent of the punk style was to shock, and tattoos and body piercings became a part of the shocking punk style. While some had colorful pictures that were personally meaningful placed on their bodies, many chose stark black tribal designs, such as Celtic knots, tattooed around the arm or ankle.

Though many people still consider tattoos to be self-destructive and offensive, many more have come to see them as beautiful body art. Throughout the 1980s, 1990s, and into the twenty-first century the popularity of tattoos has continued to increase, and many mainstream youth have begun to adorn their skin with tattoos. Other stylish youth have imitated the fashion introduced by the punks, and many stores now sell temporary tattoos, which offer the tattooed look for those who wish to avoid the pain and permanence of the needle.

FOR MORE INFORMATION

Hewitt, Kim. *Mutilating the Body: Identity in Blood and Ink.* Bowling Green, OH: Bowling Green State University Press, 1997.

Rubin, Arnold. *Marks of Civilization: Artistic Transformations of the Human Body.* Los Angeles, CA: University of California Press, 1995.

Steward, Samuel M. *Bad Boys and Tough Tattoos: A Social History of the Tattoo with Gangs, Sailors and Street-Corner Punks, 1950–1965.* Binghamton, NY: Haworth Press, 1990.

[*See also* **Volume 2, Early Asian Cultures: Tattooing; Volume 2, Oceania: Tattooing; Volume 2, Native American Cultures: Tattooing**]

Footwear, 1980–2003

The emphasis on business attire that went along with the 1980s trend for "power dressing," or dressing for business success, triggered a surge in the fashion for stiff, formal shoes. Men wore shiny leather wing tips, oxfords, and other styles, and women wore pumps to work. Some of these dressy styles were uncomfortable, and people soon embraced new styles of shoes that were comfortable as well as fashionable. Before the 1980s comfortable formal shoes were often only available in styles suited to conservative, or reserved, old women and men, but with the increasing interest in sportswear, fashion shoe manufacturers began to combine comfort with style, making classically styled shoes with flexible supportive soles.

The health craze of the 1970s that started people wearing jogging suits and tennis shoes, even when they weren't exercising, continued into the twenty-first century when people wore fashionable brand name trainer shoes, tennis shoes, and sport-specific exercise shoes at the gym, at home, and even at work. Trainer shoes became coveted fashion items for young and old alike. By the 1990s more types of athletic footwear received attention, and many young men and women began wearing hiking boots as casual, everyday boots.

The past had a great influence on the footwear styles from the 1980s to 2003. Retro styles from the 1920s (T-strap sandals), 1960s (Birkenstocks), and 1970s (platform shoes) have all reemerged on the feet of fashion-conscious people. At the beginning of the twenty-first century fashion had become a globally influenced industry, and footwear styles of the West influenced those in the East and vice versa.

FOR MORE INFORMATION

Ewing, Elizabeth. *History of Twentieth Century Fashion.* Revised by Alice Mackrell. Lanham, MD: Barnes and Noble Books, 1992.

Cowboy Boots

Cowboy boots arrived in the American West from Mexico, and they had been brought to Mexico by the Spanish horsemen who conquered that country. With sharply pointed toes and a high, angled heel, usually from one-and-a-half to two-and-a-half inches high, the tall leather boots slid easily into stirrups and hooked there when a horseman had to stand up in the saddle to rope cows. Early cowboy boots were difficult to walk in, because they were designed for use on horseback. However, even after cars and trucks replaced horses for transportation and work in the West, cowboy boots remained the footwear of choice, becoming a symbol of identity for westerners. In western states cowboy boots are even commonly worn with business suits. The forty-third U.S. president, George W. Bush (1946–), who came from Texas, favored cowboy boots for casual as well as more formal attire.

Cowboy boots are a fashion statement as well as a symbol of the American West. *Reproduced by permission of © David Stoecklein/ CORBIS.*

During the 1940s cowboy boots were in fashion for a brief time, thanks to the popularity of western films at the time, but it was the 1980 film *Urban Cowboy* that made cowboy boots fashionable street wear worldwide. Both women and men wore cowboy boots, because they seemingly portrayed a tough, masculine image yet were highly decorative. In the United States, cowboy boots became part of a nostalgic celebration of American pride, while in Europe and Asia people wore cowboy boots as a symbol of their adoption of American styles. The prime time soap opera *Dallas,* which aired on CBS from 1978 to 1991, also helped spread the popularity of the cowboy look, including, of course, stitched-leather, pointy-toed cowboy boots.

Though cowboy boots have remained popular in the American West, their popularity throughout the rest of the world had faded by the 1990s. However, the twenty-first century has seen a revival of the fashion for cowboy boots, especially in Europe, with designer boots made in bright colors, such as pink and turquoise, and using such nontraditional materials as fake fur and sequins.

Historically a young girl's shoe made of black leather, Mary Janes are now worn by women as well and can be found in a variety of colors. *Reproduced by permission of © Darama/CORBIS.*

FOR MORE INFORMATION

Fiegehen, Gary, and Jim Skipp. *Cowboy: The Legend and the Legacy.* Vancouver, British Columbia: Greystone Books, 2000.

Haskett, Tim. "How the West Won: The Cowboy Boot's Ride From Prairie to Pret-a-Porter." *Footwear News* (April 17, 1995): 67–69.

■ Mary Janes

Mary Janes, also called bar shoes, are simple, flat-soled shoes with bars, or straps, across the instep that fasten with a buckle or button, and, for more recent styles, with Velcro. A common style of children's shoe since before the twentieth century, Mary Janes became popular among women in the late twentieth century.

Bar shoes became known as Mary Janes after the Brown Shoe Company of Missouri began marketing the shoes named after the popular cartoon character Buster Brown and his sister Mary Jane in 1904. While Mary Janes have remained popular young girls' footwear, adult women began to wear them in the 1960s. In the early twenty-first century, chunky, thick-soled styles of Mary Janes made by Simple Shoes of California were worn by trendy young women, while more delicate designs made of supple leather and thin, feminine bars were worn by some women for work and casual wear. Historically made of black leather, by the twenty-first century Mary Janes came in a variety of colors, some with embroidery and patterns.

FOR MORE INFORMATION

"Our History." *Brown Shoe Company.* http://www.brownshoe.com/history/index.asp (accessed on August 27, 2003).

Pumps

Pumps, low-cut, slip-on shoes, developed from the shoes worn at royal courts in Europe in the 1870s and have been popular in a variety of versions ever since. The earliest varieties had thick one- to two-inch heels. But after World War II (1939–45) women embraced ultrafeminine styles and wore pumps with higher, slimmer heels. By the 1950s women teetered on pointy-toed pumps with four-inch-high stiletto heels. But throughout the 1960s and 1970s pumps became more practical for walking, with lower, thicker heels and rounded or squared toes.

The 1980s version of the pump was sleek, featuring a U-shaped throat (the opening for the foot), a pointed toe, and a stiletto heel, resembling the style first popularized in the 1950s. The feminine styling and high heel of the pump contrasted with the masculine styling of the tailored suits women wore to work. The combination came to symbolize women's newfound power on the job. The only problem was that these pumps were terribly uncomfortable. Working women soon began seeking lower-heeled pumps for work. The more casual styles of the 1990s brought thicker heels and squared or rounded toes to pumps made in a variety of fabrics, from stiff leather to elasticized cloth. By the twenty-first century the pointed-toe, stiletto heeled pump had returned to favor.

FOR MORE INFORMATION

Cosgrave, Bronwyn. *The Complete History of Costume and Fashion: From Ancient Egypt to the Present Day.* New York: Checkmark Books, 2000.

Lawlor, Laurie. *Where Will This Shoe Take You?: A Walk Through the History of Footwear.* New York: Walker and Co., 1996.

Pratt, Lucy, and Linda Woolley. *Shoes.* London, England: V&A Publications, 1999.

[*See also* **Volume 5, 1946–60: Stiletto Heel**]

A brown alligator-skin pump. Pumps have been an essential style of footwear for more than one hundred years. *Reproduced by permission of © Royalty-Free/ CORBIS.*

Trainer Shoes

During the 1980s sneakers or athletic shoes became a major component of the American wardrobe. Consumers, most of whom were young, favored certain styles for the attitude or personality they conveyed. Wearing a specific brand or style radiated status. One of the most distinctive styles of athletic shoe introduced in the 1980s was the trainer. Not designed for a specific sport such as basketball or jogging, trainers typically had heavier soles, more decorative and colorful uppers, and prominent display of the shoe-maker's logo. While traditional sneakers came in such colors as black, white, blue, or red, trainers could be a less typical color, such as pink. The shoes' laces were often colored and patterned or replaced by Velcro strips.

For decades rubber-soled athletic shoes, also known as tennis shoes and sneakers, had been worn primarily by children romping on playgrounds and athletes competing in sports and were considered inappropriate for work or school. The most well-known brands were Keds and Converse "Chuck Taylor" All-Stars. By the 1980s, however, more people of all ages began exercising and participating in sports, and shoe manufactures began designing different types of sneakers for different athletic activities: one style for jogging, another for tennis, and a third for basketball.

As sales figures skyrocketed, marketers realized that athletic shoes could be sold to the style-conscious as well as the sports-

NIKE: THE FASHION OF SPORTS

One of the largest and best-known sellers of sportswear in the world, Nike began as a maker of athletic shoes, then branched out into shoes and clothes for athletes and those who wanted to dress like athletes. The company started during the mid-1960s, just in time to take advantage of a national fitness craze, which inspired average people to buy specialized sports shoes and clothes. Most of those who spend millions of dollars each year to buy this specialized sportswear never take part in the sport for which their apparel was designed. However, since the late 1970s fitness has been in fashion, and it is almost as fashionable to dress like an athlete as it is to be one.

Nike was founded by two athletes seeking to improve athletic footwear. Bill Bowerman (1909–) was track coach at the University of Oregon and Phil Knight (1938–) was an accounting student he had coached. They sought good quality inexpensive shoes for runners and found them in Japan. In 1962 they formed a company, Blue Ribbon Sports, and began to import Japanese track shoes, selling them at track meets from the

trunks of their cars. Bowerman began experimenting with shoe designs himself, and by 1966 Bowerman, Knight, and others formed their own manufacturing company, which they named Nike, for the Greek goddess of victory. A graphic arts student at the University of Oregon named Carolyn Davidson designed a logo for the new company, a simple "swoosh," a curved shape that suggested motion.

Success came quickly to the new shoe company. In 1967 Bowerman wrote a book about a new form of exercise for the average person called "jogging." The idea became popular and suddenly running was not just for track stars anymore. In 1974 Nike introduced its now famous "waffle trainer," the sole of which Bowerman had created by pouring latex into a waffle iron, and joggers everywhere began to buy the specialized running shoes.

Nike took advantage of this trend with a series of clever, innovative ads for their products. Nike advertisements did not focus on their products; in many ads the products were not pictured. Instead, they showed the attitude and lifestyle of the athlete, overcoming obstacles, trying hard to win. Slogans like "Just Do It" drew in customers who might not be athletic but wanted to be strong, at-

minded. Sneakers could be everyday fashion statements. Some of the fashionable trainers included KangaROOS, which featured small pockets for holding trinkets; L.A. Gear, which marketed high-top sneakers called Brats that had oversized tongues, the loose fabric that lies under a shoe's laces. Brats were worn with loosely tied laces, allowing the tongue to be visible. Young children favored Velcro trainers featuring colored patches that glowed in the dark.

Brand name trainers became popular with the help of celebrities. Adidas trainers featuring shell-shaped toes made of white rubber were popularized by members of the rap group Run-DMC; rap artists LL Cool J (1968–) and MC Hammer (1962–) exclusively wore Troop trainers. Trainers of all sorts, including the more athletically oriented cross-trainer, continue to be worn by men and

tractive, and successful like the Nike athletes. Nike also chose a rebellious image for many of its products, which also appealed to young professionals of the late 1970s and early 1980s. Nike spokespeople have often been energetic athletes with big personalities, such as basketball's Michael Jordan (1963–), tennis's John McEnroe (1959–), and figure skating's Tonya Harding (1970–).

In 1979 Nike began to market athletic clothing as well as shoes. Along with outfitting hundreds of teams worldwide, the Nike swoosh was now seen on the street clothes of millions of individuals. Nike continued to work with fashion designers and bought innovative shoe design companies such as Cole-Haan Shoes, in order to keep its clothing and shoes on the cutting edge of style. In the mid-1990s Nike opened Nike Town, a new kind of superstore. Filled with special features such as basketball courts, video theaters, aquariums, and sound effects of sports events and cheering crowds, Nike Town was designed to make the customer feel a part of an exciting athletic lifestyle. By 2003 there were thirteen Nike Towns in major cities around the world, and in 2001 the company opened the first NikeGoddess store to sell fashionable sportswear for women only.

The Nike swoosh is a common sight on and off the track. *Reproduced by permission of © P. Pichon/CORBIS SYGMA.*

women in everyday use into the twenty-first century, alongside the more specialized running, basketball, and other sport-specific shoes that make up the larger sneaker market.

FOR MORE INFORMATION

Greenberg, Keith Elliot. *Bill Bowerman and Phil Knight: Building the Nike Empire.* Woodbridge, CT: Blackbirch Press, 1994.

Hays, Scott. *The Story of Nike.* Mankato, MN: Smart Apple Media, 2000.

Strasser, J. B., and Laurie Becklund. *Swoosh: The Unauthorized Story of Nike and the Men Who Played There.* New York: HarperInformation, 1993.

Vanderbilt, Tom. *The Sneaker Book: Anatomy of an Industry and an Icon.* New York: New Press, 1998.

Woods, Samuel G. *Sneakers from Start to Finish.* Woodbridge, CT: Blackbirch Press, 1999.

Where to Learn More

■ ■ ■

The following list of resources focuses on material appropriate for middle school or high school students. Please note that Web site addresses were verified prior to publication but are subject to change.

BOOKS

Batterberry, Michael, and Ariane Batterberry. *Fashion: The Mirror of History.* New York: Greenwich House, 1977.

Bigelow, Marybelle S. *Fashion in History: Apparel in the Western World.* Minneapolis, MN: Burgess Publishing, 1970.

Boucher, François. *20,000 Years of Fashion: The History of Costume and Personal Adornment.* Extended ed. New York: Harry N. Abrams, 1987.

Contini, Mila. *Fashion: From Ancient Egypt to the Present Day.* Edited by James Laver. New York: Odyssey Press, 1965.

Corson, Richard. *Fashions in Hair: The First Five Thousand Years.* London, England: Peter Owen, 2001.

Cosgrave, Bronwyn. *The Complete History of Costume and Fashion: From Ancient Egypt to the Present Day.* New York: Checkmark Books, 2000.

Ewing, Elizabeth; revised and updated by Alice Mackrell. *History of Twentieth Century Fashion.* Lanham, MD: Barnes and Noble Books, 1992.

Hoobler, Dorothy, and Thomas Hoobler. *Vanity Rules: A History of American Fashion and Beauty.* Brookfield, CT: Twenty-First Century Books, 2000.

Laver, James. *Costume and Fashion: A Concise History.* 4th ed. London, England: Thames and Hudson, 2002.

Lawlor, Laurie. *Where Will This Shoe Take You?: A Walk through the History of Footwear.* New York: Walker and Co., 1996.

Lister, Margot. *Costume: An Illustrated Survey from Ancient Times to the Twentieth Century.* London, England: Herbert Jenkins, 1967.

Miller, Brandon Marie. *Dressed for the Occasion: What Americans Wore 1620-1970.* Minneapolis, MN: Lerner Publications, 1999.

Mulvagh, Jane. *Vogue History of 20th Century Fashion.* New York: Viking, 1988.

Payne, Blanche, Geitel Winakor, and Jane Farrell-Beck. *The History of Costume.* 2nd ed. New York: HarperCollins, 1992.

Peacock, John. *The Chronicle of Western Fashion: From Ancient Times to the Present Day.* New York: Harry N. Abrams, 1991.

Perl, Lila. *From Top Hats to Baseball Caps, from Bustles to Blue Jeans: Why We Dress the Way We Do.* New York: Clarion Books, 1990.

Pratt, Lucy, and Linda Woolley. *Shoes.* London, England: V&A Publications, 1999.

Racinet, Auguste. *The Historical Encyclopedia of Costumes.* New York: Facts on File, 1988.

Ribeiro, Aileen. *The Gallery of Fashion.* Princeton, NJ: Princeton University Press, 2000.

Rowland-Warne, L. *Costume.* New York: Dorling Kindersley, 2000.

Schnurnberger, Lynn Edelman. *Let There Be Clothes: 40,000 Years of Fashion.* New York: Workman, 1991.

Schoeffler, O. E., and William Gale. *Esquire's Encyclopedia of 20th Century Men's Fashions.* New York: McGraw-Hill, 1973.

Sichel, Marion. *History of Men's Costume.* New York: Chelsea House, 1984.

Steele, Valerie. *Fifty Years of Fashion: New Look to Now.* New Haven, CT: Yale University Press, 1997.

Trasko, Mary. *Daring Do's: A History of Extraordinary Hair.* New York: Flammarion, 1994.

Yarwood, Doreen. *The Encyclopedia of World Costume.* New York: Charles Scribner's Sons, 1978.

Yarwood, Doreen. *Fashion in the Western World, 1500–1990.* New York: Drama Book Publishers, 1992.

WEB SITES

Bender, A. *La Couturière Parisienne.* http://marquise.de/index.html (accessed on September 10, 2003).

Kathie Rothkop Hair Design. *Hair History.* http://www.hairrific.com/hist.htm (accessed on September 10, 2003).

Ladnier, Penny D. Dunlap. *The Costume Gallery.* http://www.costume gallery.com (accessed on September 10, 2003).

Maginnis, Tara. *The Costumer's Manifesto.* http://www.costumes.org/ (accessed on September 10, 2003).

Metropolitan Museum of Art. *The Costume Institute.* http://www. metmuseum.org/collections/department.asp?dep=8 (accessed on September 10, 2003).

Museum of Costume, Bath. http://www.museumofcostume.co.uk (accessed on September 10, 2003).

Sardo, Julie Zetterberg. *The Costume Page: Costuming Resources Online.* http://members.aol.com/nebula5/costume.html (accessed on September 10, 2003).

Thomas, Pauline Weston, and Guy Thomas. *Fashion-Era.* http://www. fashion-era.com/index.htm (accessed on September 10, 2003).

Index

■ ■ ■

Italic type indicates volume number; **boldface** type indicates main entries and then page numbers; (ill.) indicates photos and illustrations.

A

C

D

H

K

M

Polar fleece, *5:* **990–92**, 991 (ill.)
Polo, *5:* 976
Polo shirt, *4:* **797–98**
Polonaise style, *3:* **567–68**, 567 (ill.)
Pomanders, *3:* 493–94, 495
Pompadour, *4:* **821–22**
Pompadour, Madame de, *3:* 575–76
Poniewaz, Jeff, *5:* 942
Popular culture, *4:* 660. *See also* specific people and movies
Porkpie hats, *5:* 867
Porosknit, *4:* 691
Porsche, *5:* 972
Postal services, *3:* 602
Postwar fashion. *See* 1946–1960
Potter, James, *3:* 619
Pouf, *3:* **580**
Poulaines, Crackowes and, *2:* **326–28**, 327 (ill.)
Pourpoint, *2:* **308–9**
Power dressing, *5:* 972
Pratt, Lucy, *4:* 837
Prehistory, *1:* 1–14
    body decorations, *1:* 11–12, 12 (ill.)
    clothing in, *1:* 5–8, 6 (ill.)
    Cro-Magnon man, *1:* 2–4, 2 (ill.)
    footwear, *1:* 13–14
    headwear, *1:* 9
    life, *1:* 1–2
Preppy Look, *5:* 850, **862–63**, 862 (ill.)
Presley, Elvis, *4:* 822; *5:* 865, 875, 875 (ill.)
Presley, Priscilla, *5:* 953
Priests. *See* Clergy
Prince of Wales, *4:* 678
Printing presses, *3:* 602
Prohibition, *4:* 723–24
Protective clothing. *See* Weatherproof clothing
Protestant Reformation, *3:* 466–67
Pschent, *1:* **34–35**
Public baths, *1:* 191; *2:* 269
Puka chokers, *5:* **952–53**, 952 (ill.)

Puma, *4:* 716
Pumps, *4:* 713; *5:* 883, **1018–19**, 1019 (ill.)
Punjabi suit, *1:* **83–84**, 83 (ill.)
Punk style, *5:* 900, 946–47, 947 (ill.)
Purdah, *1:* **84, 86**
Puritans, *3:* 513
Purses, *2:* **323**
    1900–1918, *4:* 705
    1980–2003, *5:* 1005
    backpack, *5:* 1006–7, 1006 (ill.)
    beaded handbags, *4:* 705, 707–8, 707 (ill.)
    clutch, *4:* 827–28, 828 (ill.)
    Gucci bags, *5:* 1007–9
    Middle Ages, *2:* 323
Puttees, *4:* 681
Pyramids, *1:* 16 (ill.), 17

Q

Qing dynasty, *2:* 207, 212, 216, 217–18, 235, 247
Quant, Mary, *5:* 899 (ill.)
    boutique, *5:* 921
    fashion show, *5:* 941
    miniskirts, *5:* 922, 928
    youthquake movement, *5:* 896–97, 898
Quicklime, *2:* 321

R

R. Griggs and Company, *5:* 961
Raccoon coat, *4:* 728, **739–40**, 741
Rachel haircut, *5:* **1001–2**, 1001 (ill.)
Racial discrimination, *5:* 890
Radiocarbon dating, *1:* 4
Radios, *4:* 723
Raft, George, *4:* 759
Ramillies, Pigtails and, *3:* **579–80**, 579 (ill.)

T

X

Y

Z